For John

MODEL AMERICAN
KATY GRANNAN

Essay by Jan Avgikos

aperture

I met E. on a sidewalk in Poughkeepsie just as her boyfriend pulled away from the curb; inside the car, their daughter was strapped into her car seat. They waved good-bye to both of us. Nearly three years later, E. called to let me know she had moved to the Catskills with her three young children. Her number was unlisted; her boyfriend had beat her up again, this time nearly killing her. She was okay, though, and wanted to be photographed again. **POUGHKEEPSIE JOURNAL**, 1998

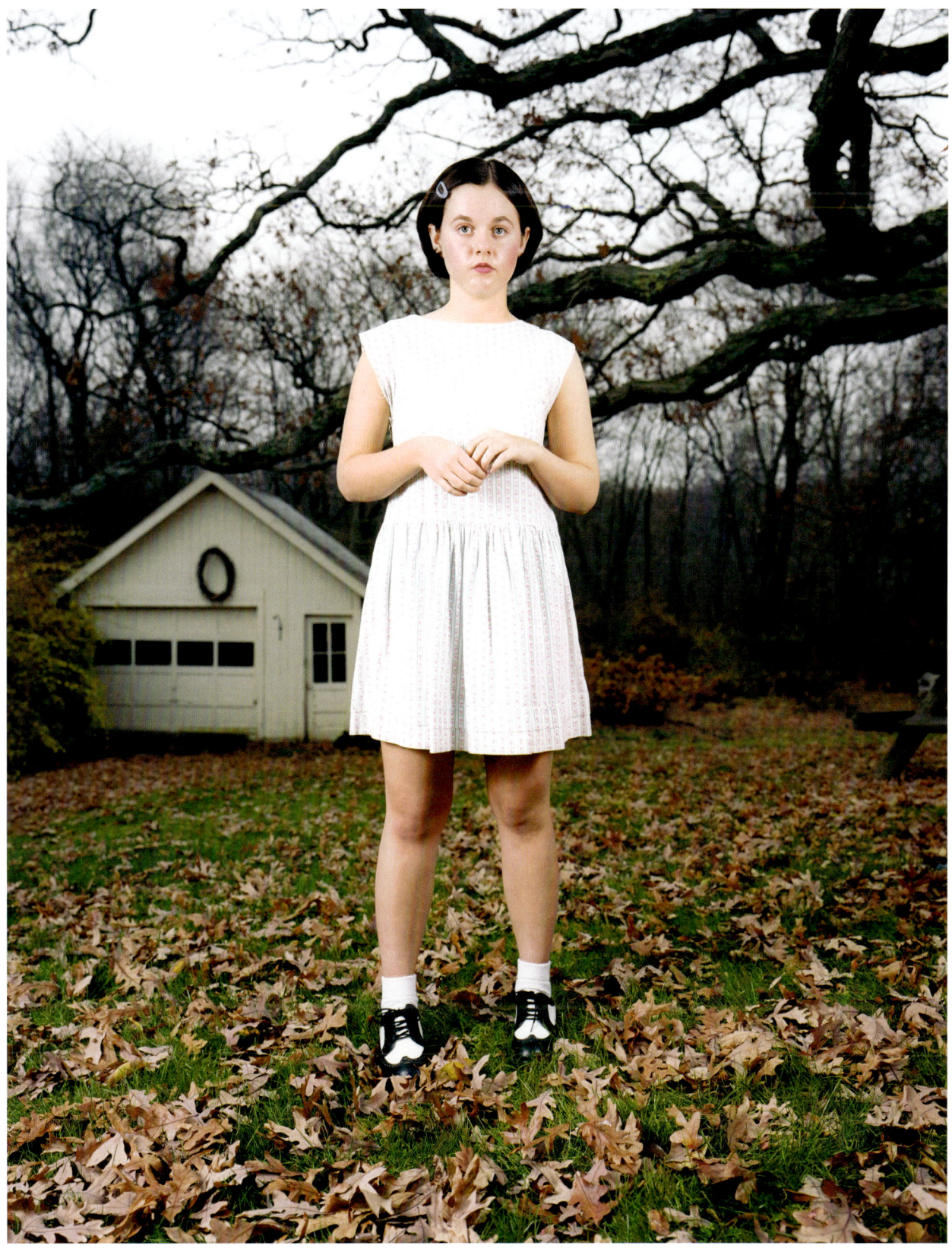

Untitled, 1998

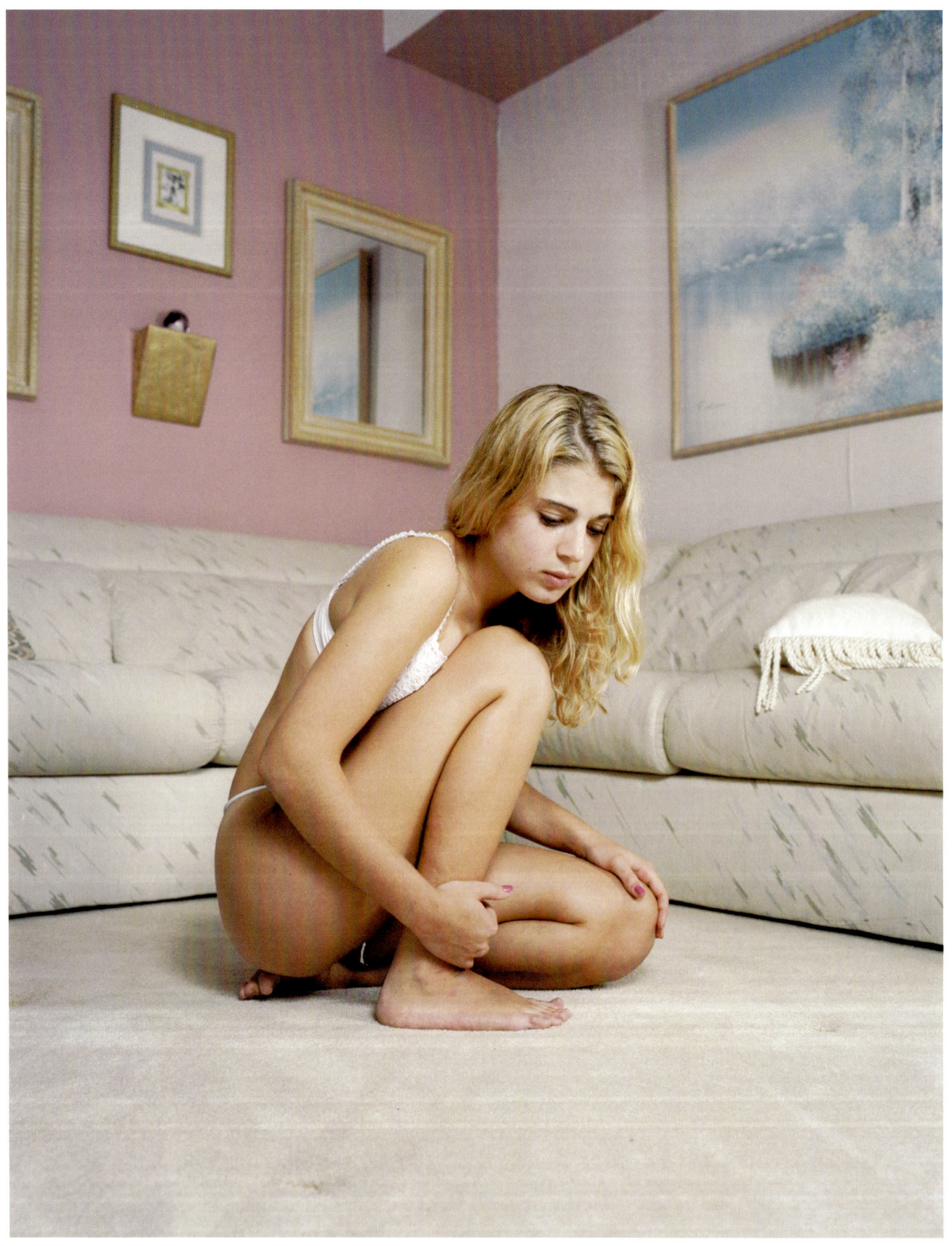

Untitled, 1998

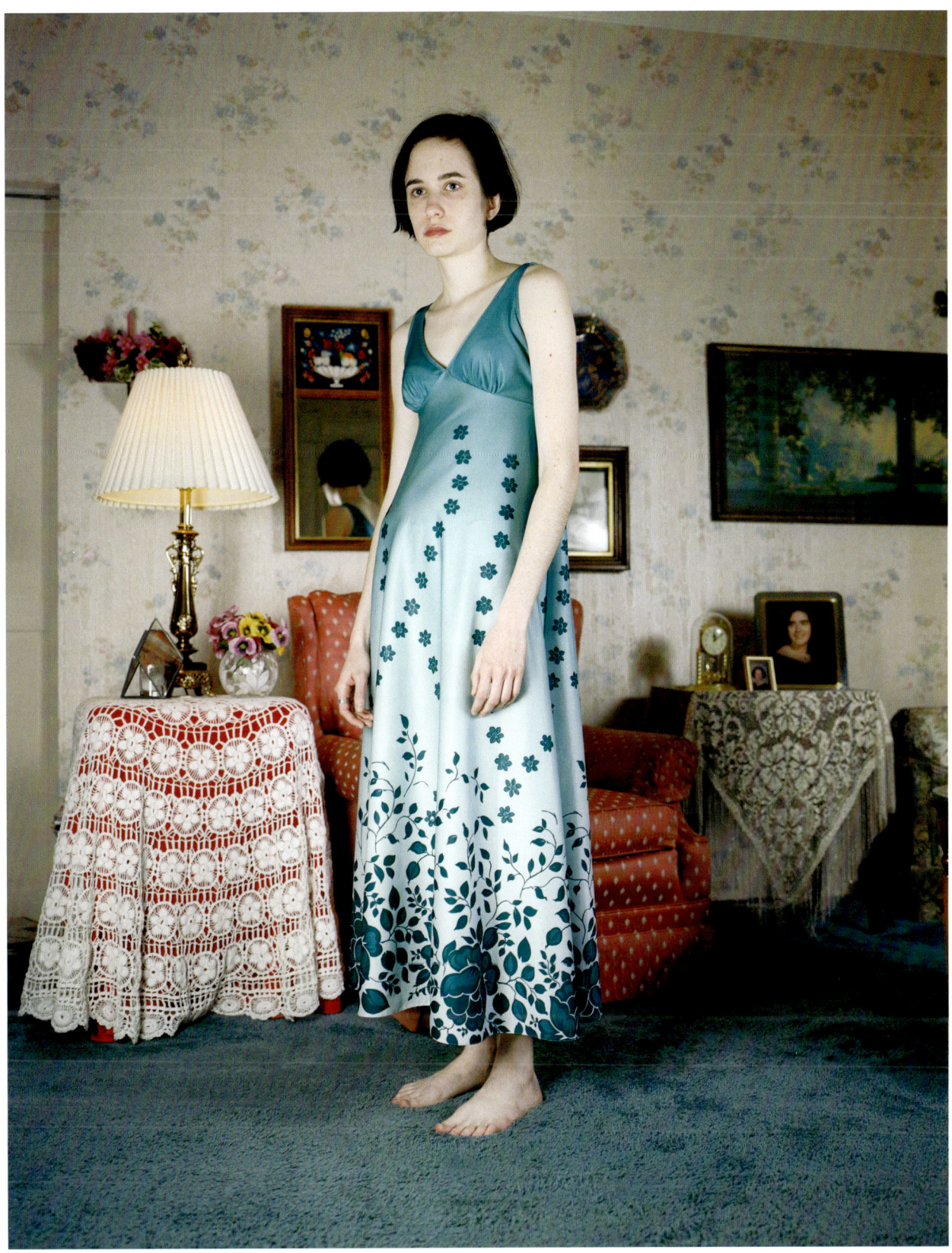

Untitled, 1998

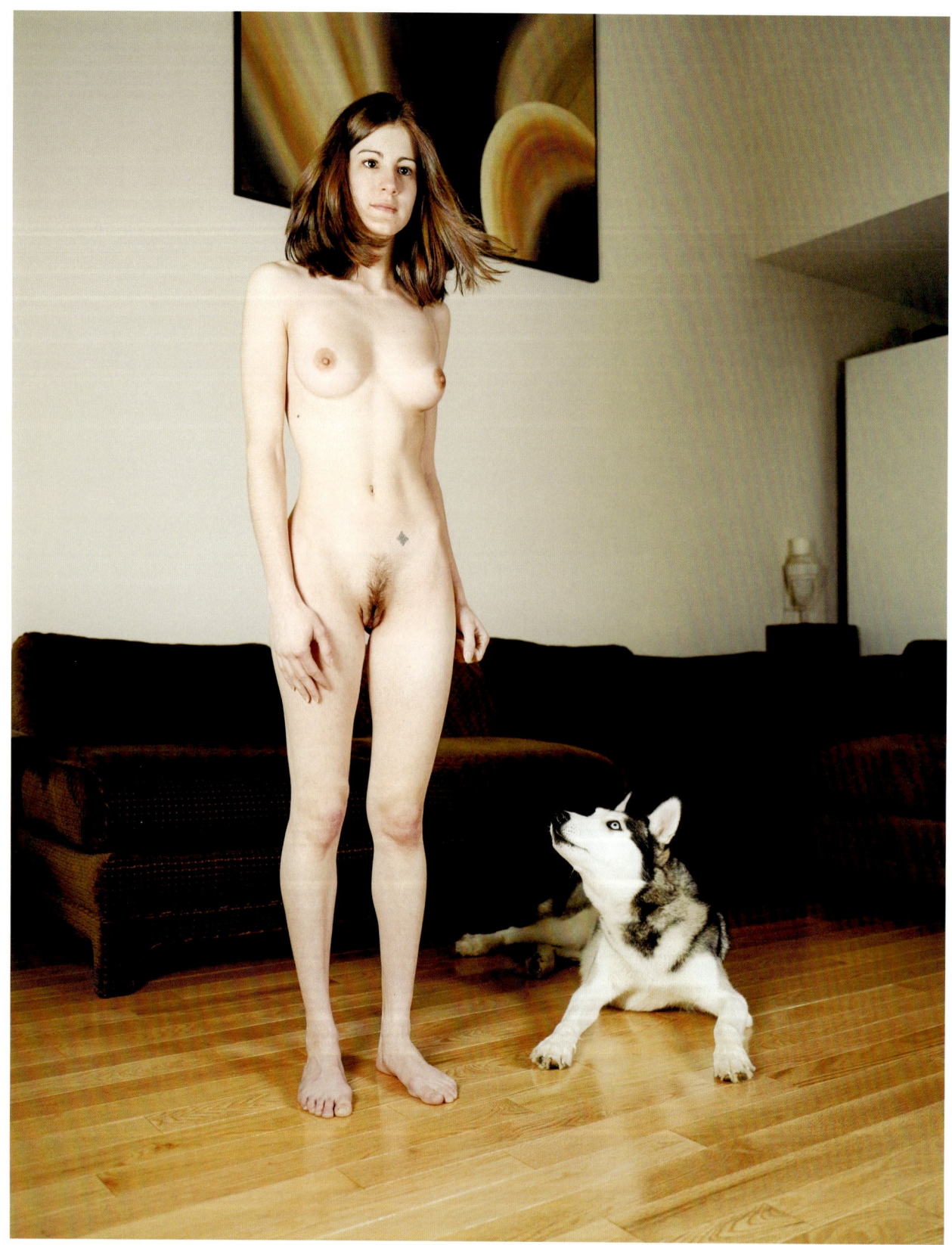

Untitled, 1998

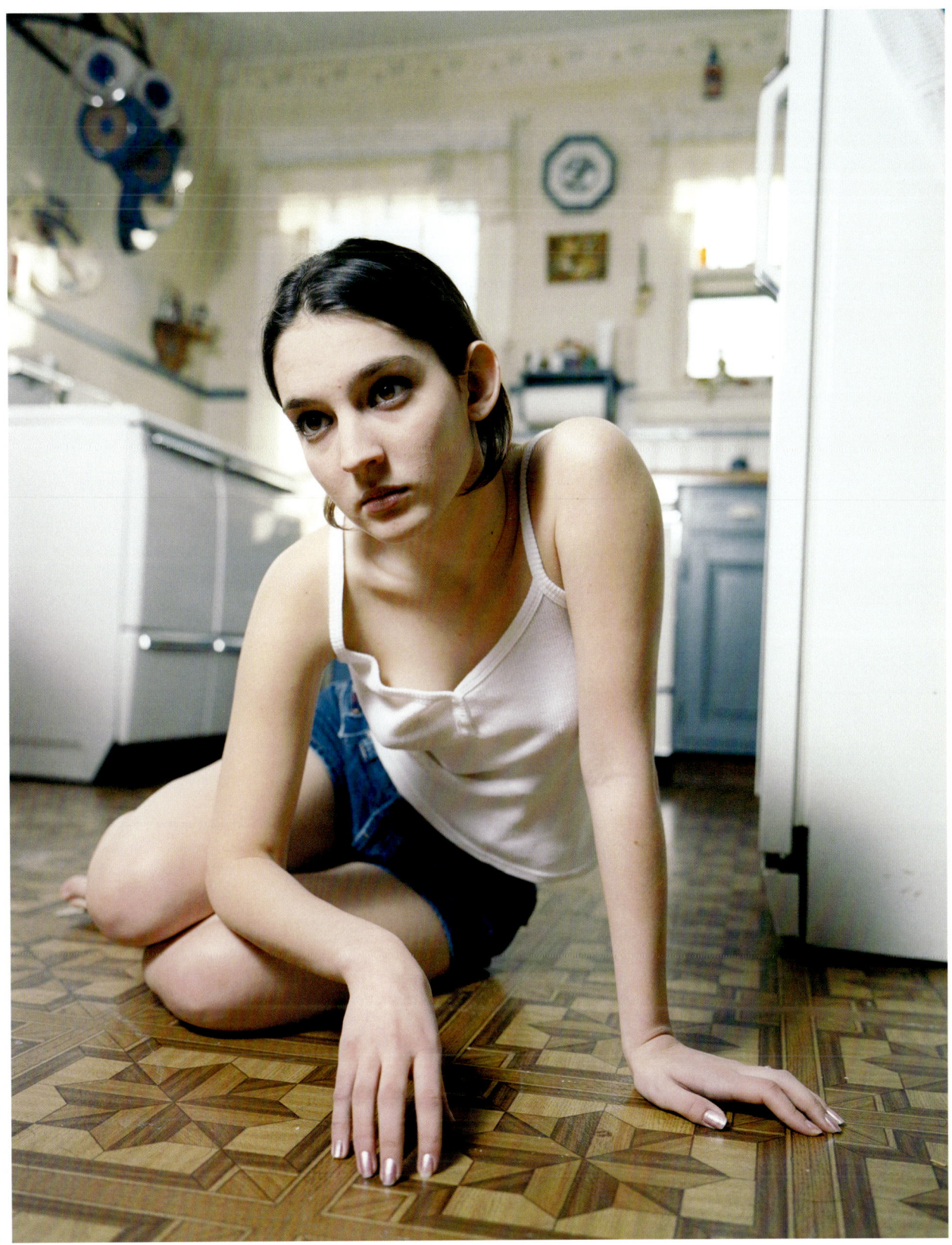

Untitled, 1999

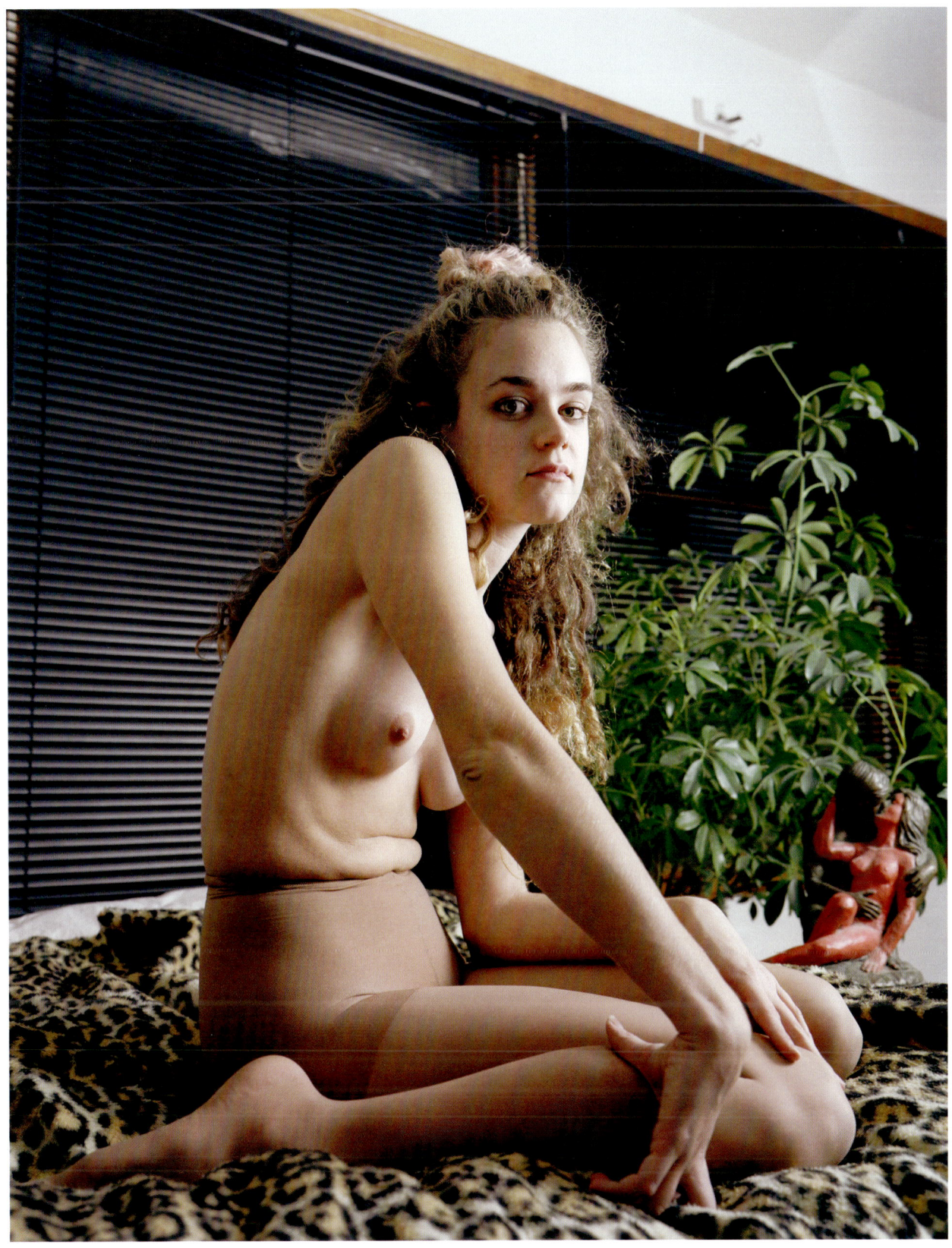

Untitled, 1998

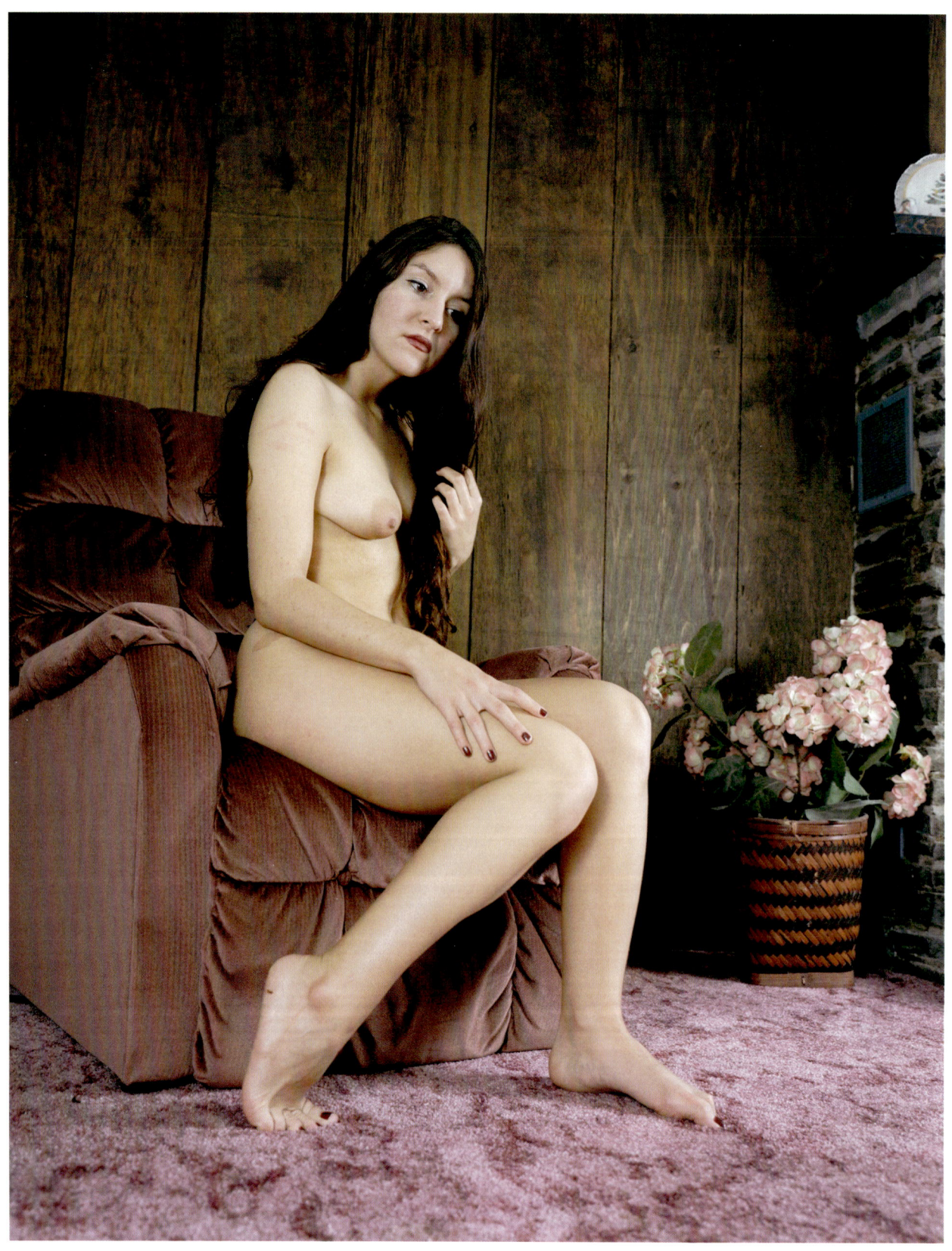

Untitled, 1998

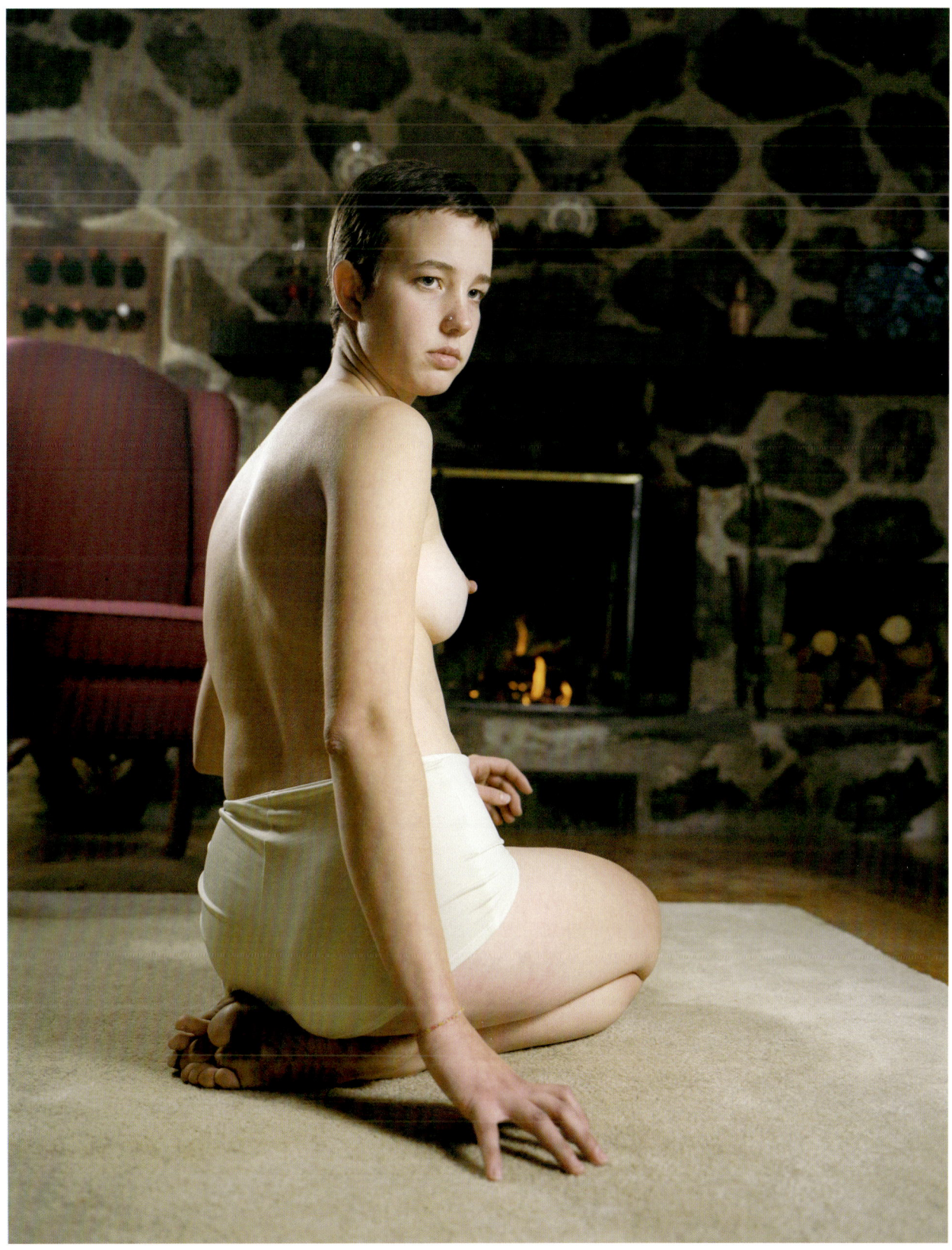

Untitled, 1998

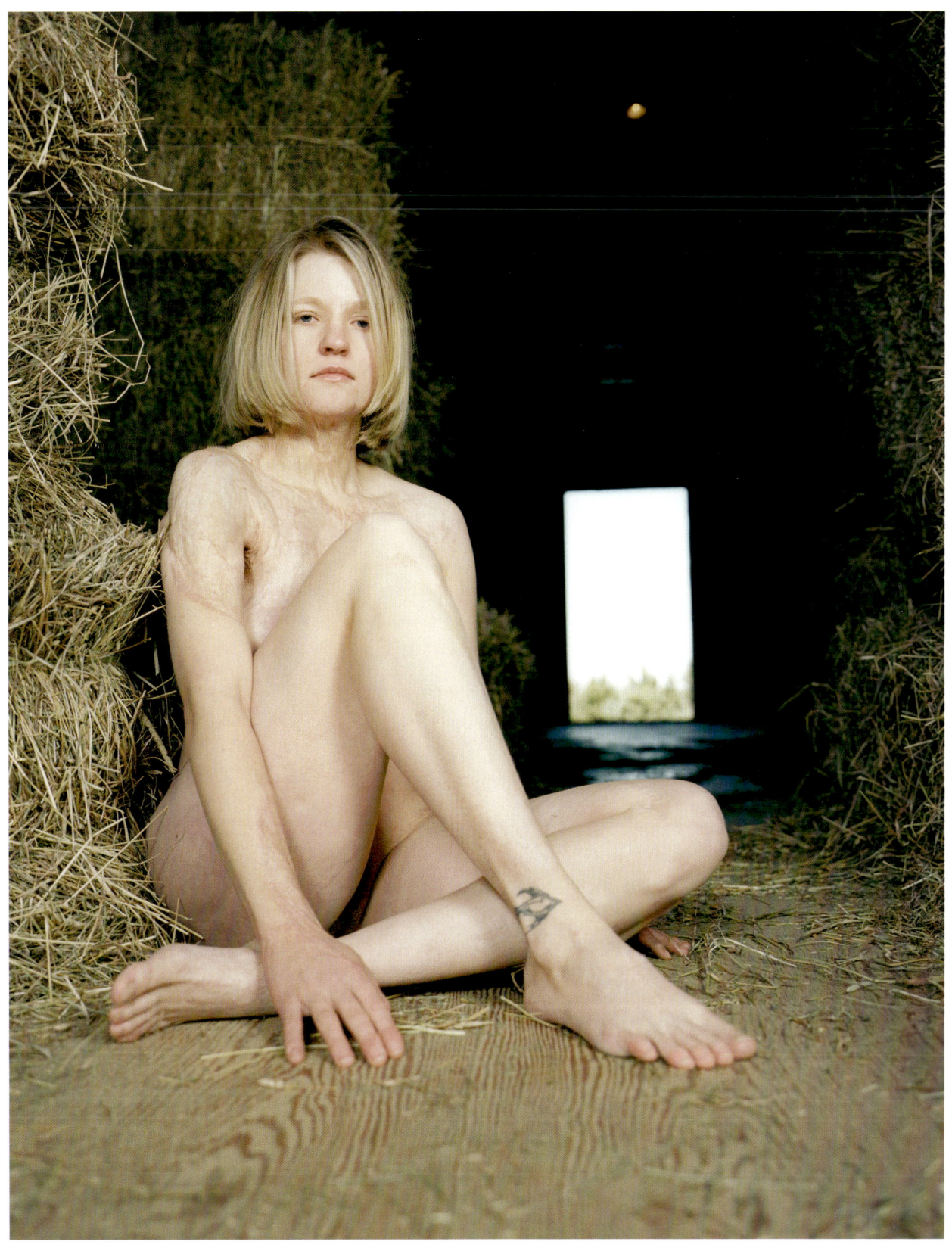

Untitled, 1998

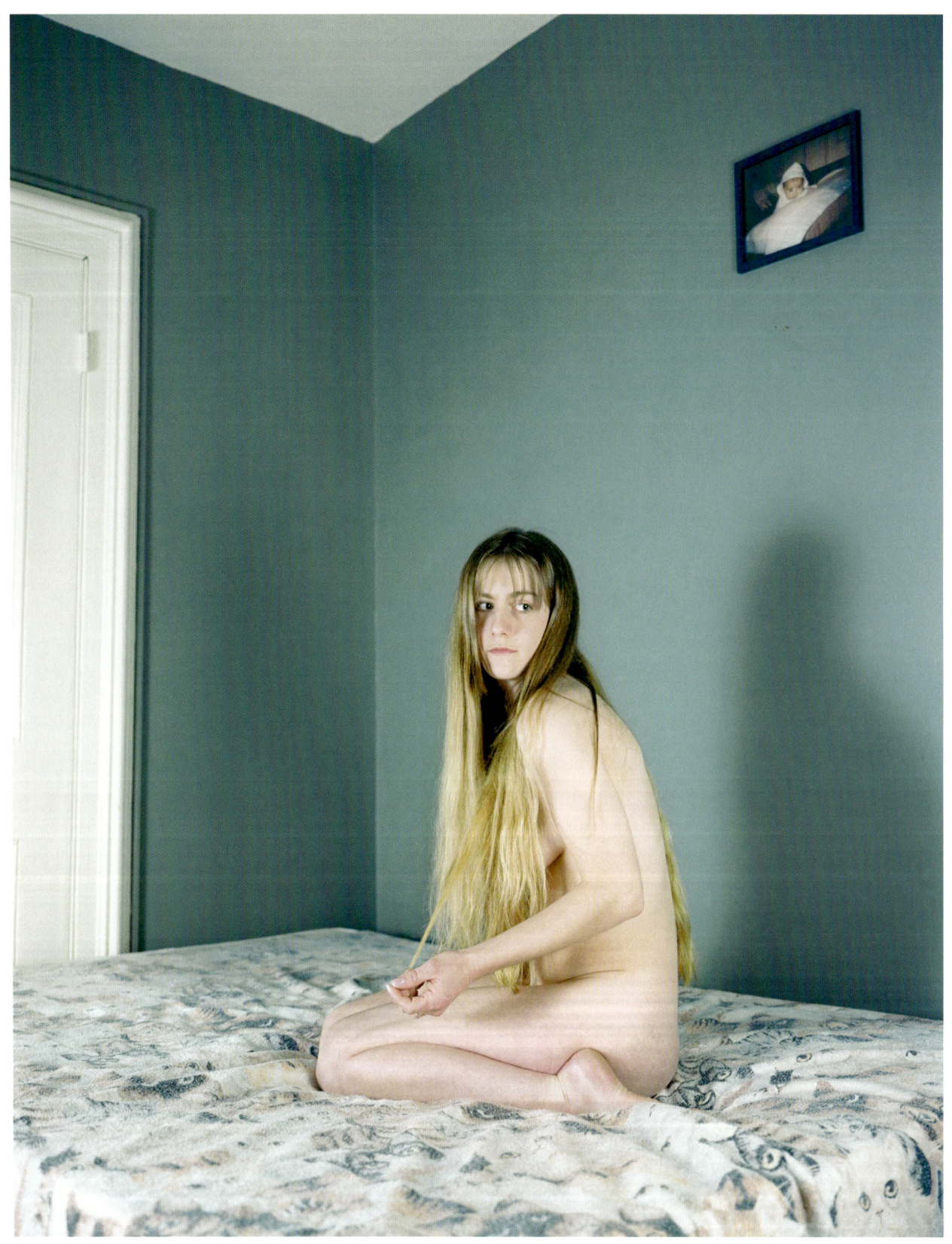

Untitled, 1998

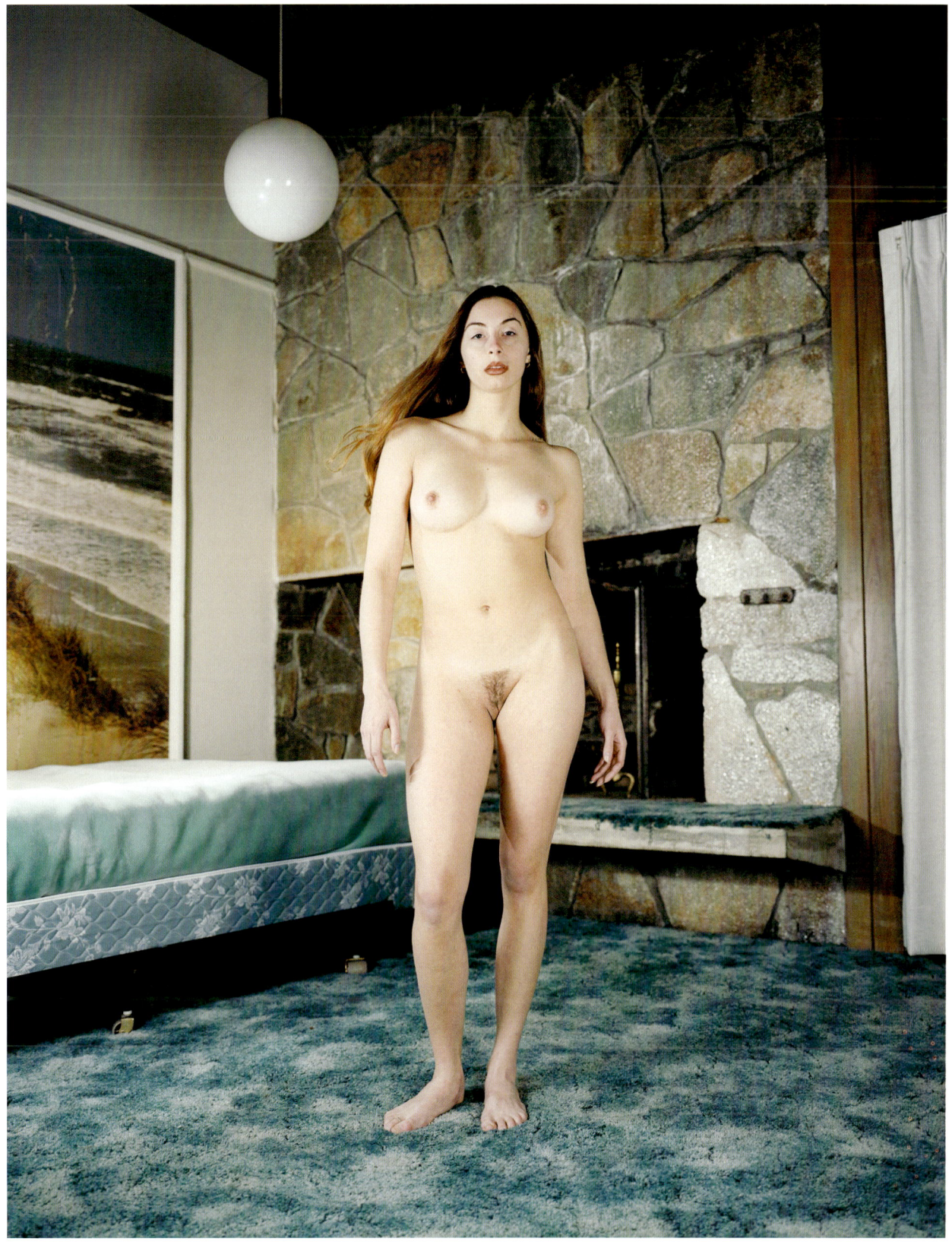

Untitled, 1998

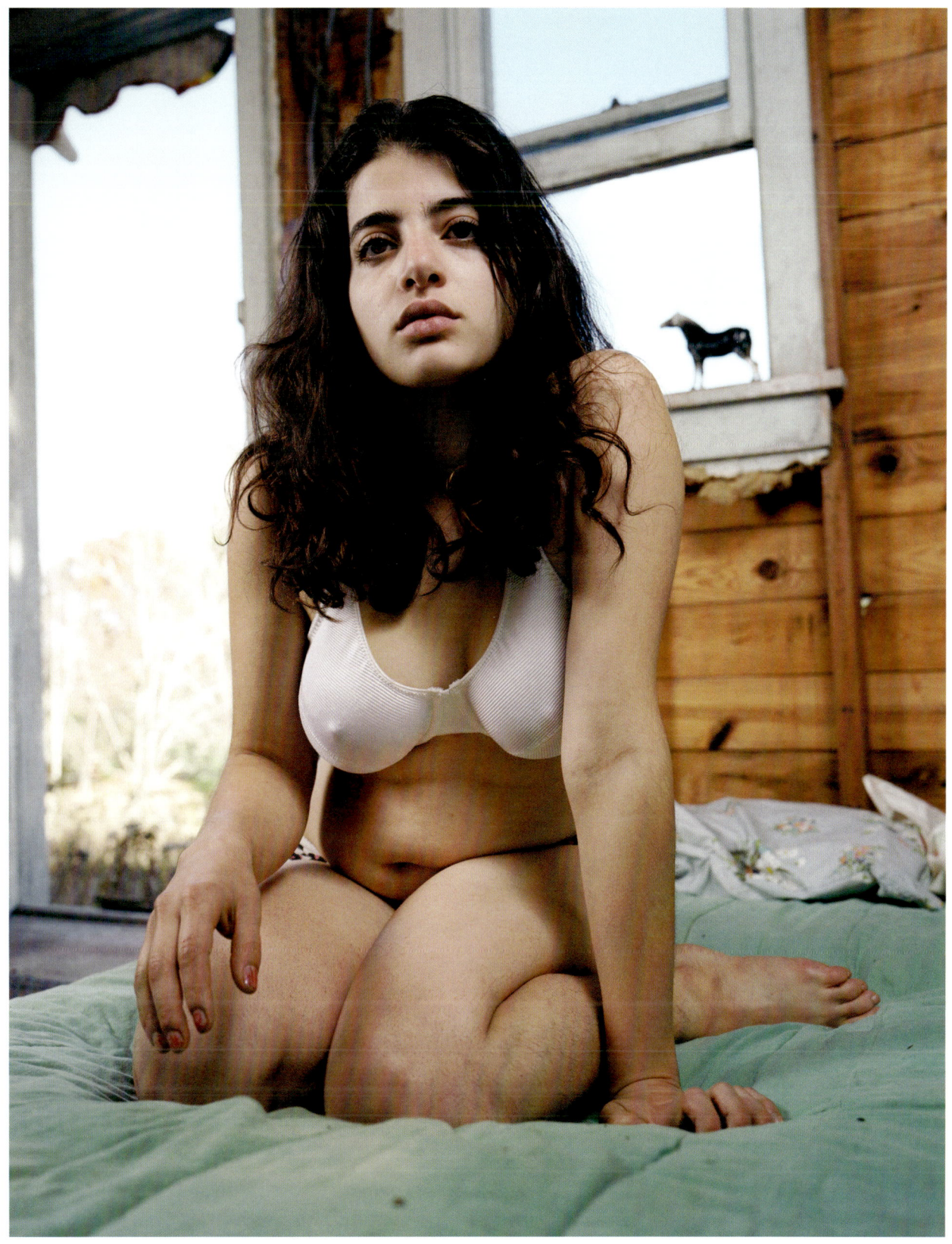

Untitled, 1998

M.'s grandmother stood over us, smoking cigarettes and asking too many questions. She told M. that she was too fat to be photographed–who did she think she was, anyway? The room had low ceilings and dingy floral wallpaper that hadn't changed since the 1950s, back when the place had been a brothel. The small bed was draped in a thin plastic cover. The air in the room grew increasingly thick and claustrophobic.   **DREAM AMERICA**, 1999-2000

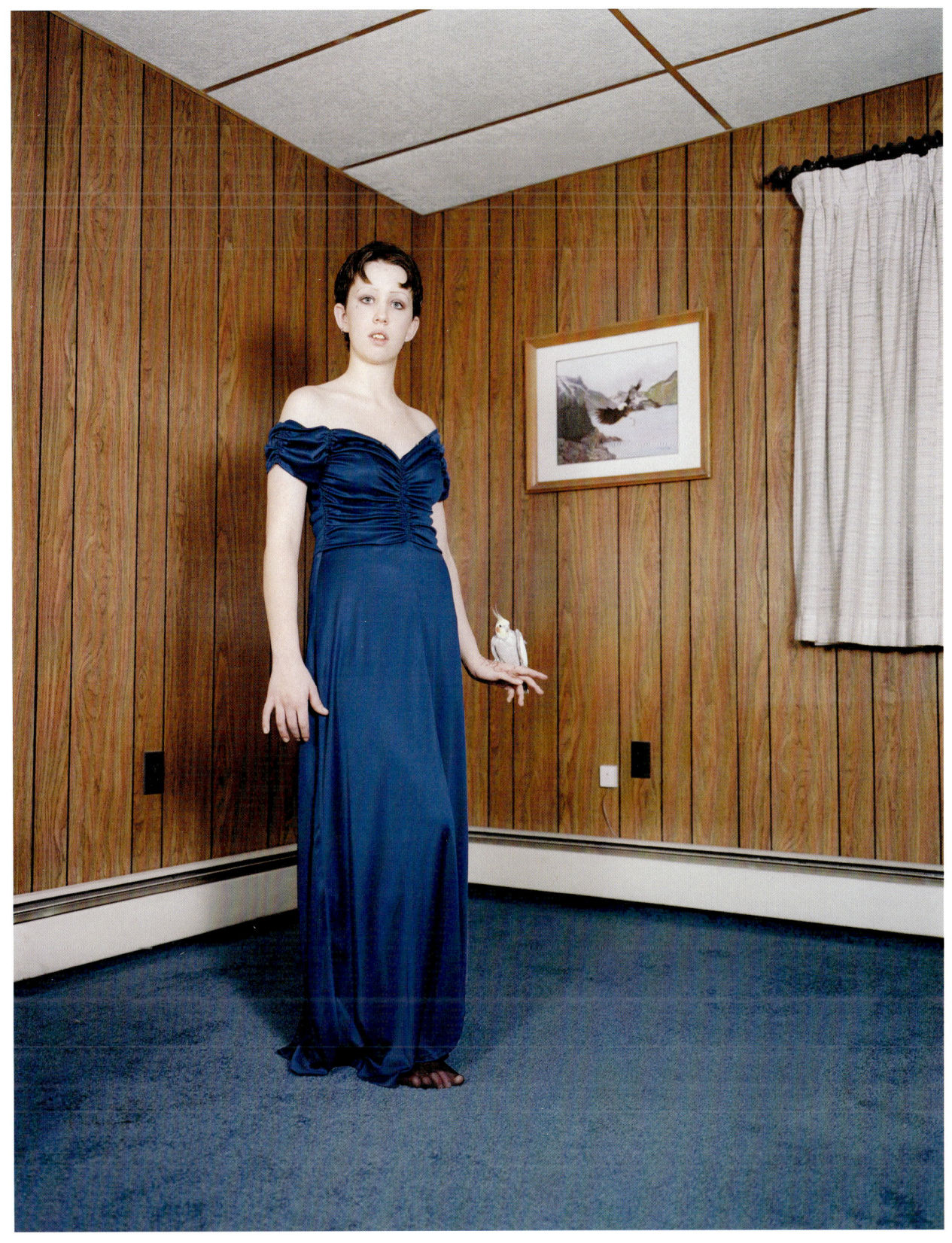

Ghent, NY, 2000

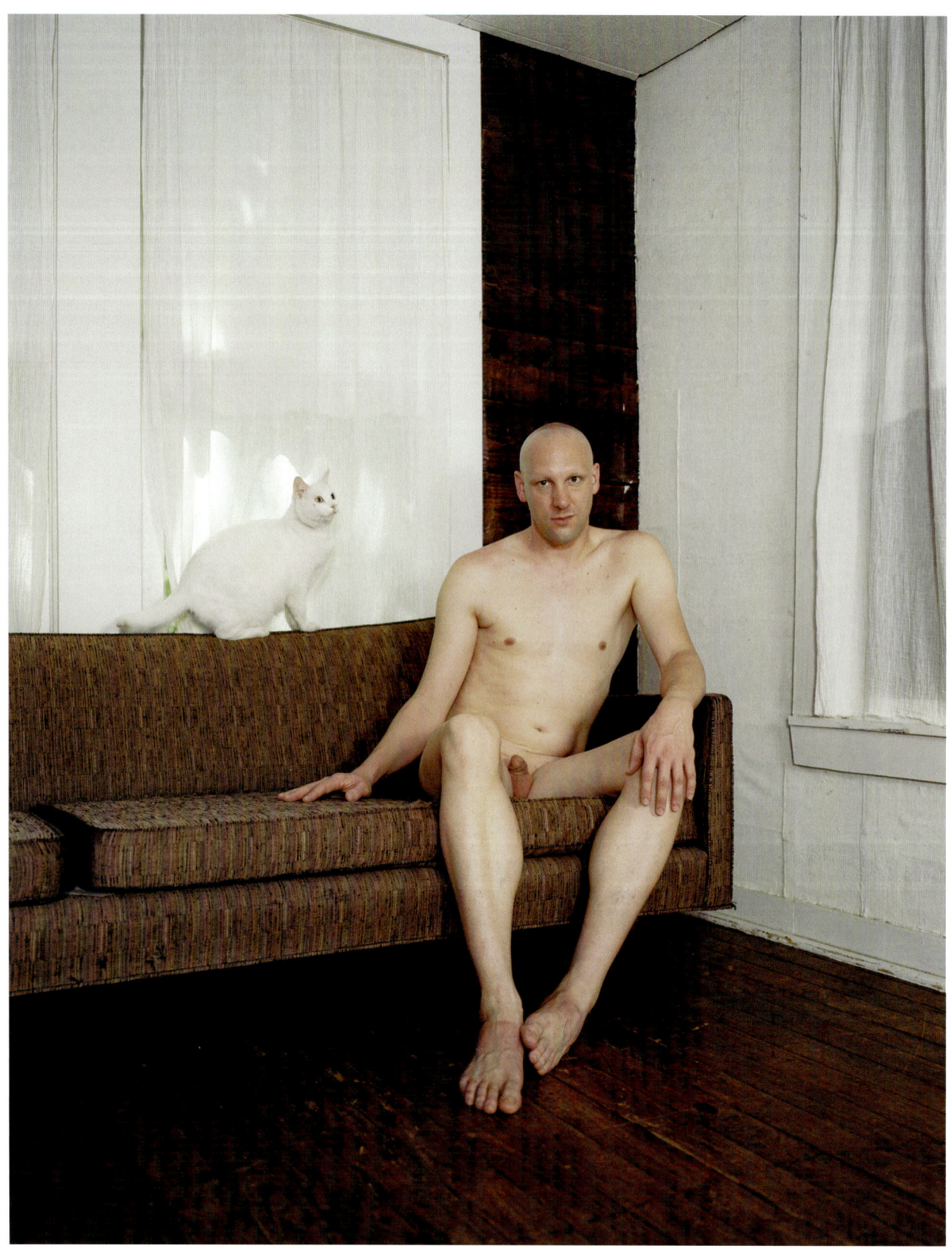

Man with Neighbor's Cat, Austin, TX, 2000

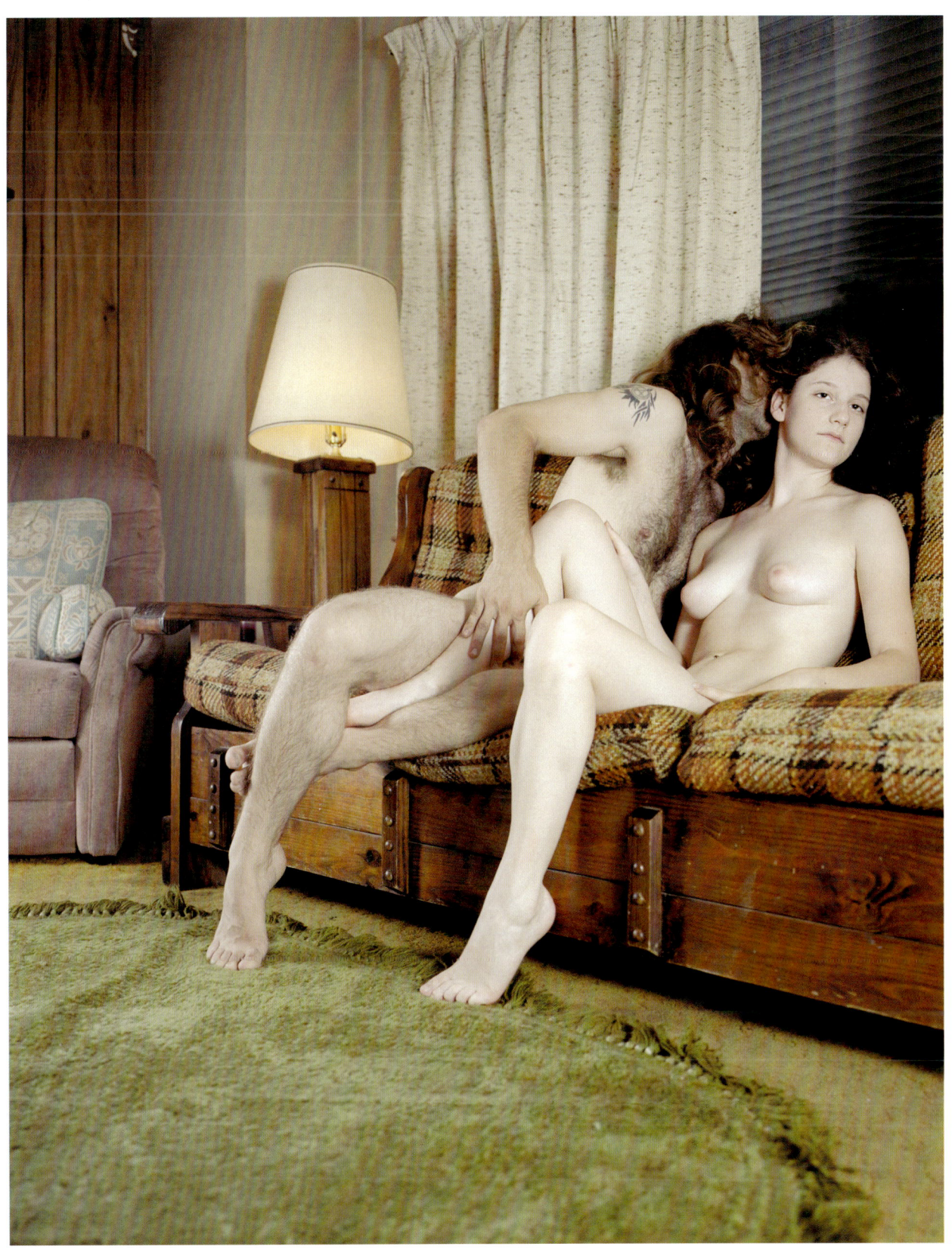

Young Couple, Hyde Park, NY, 1999

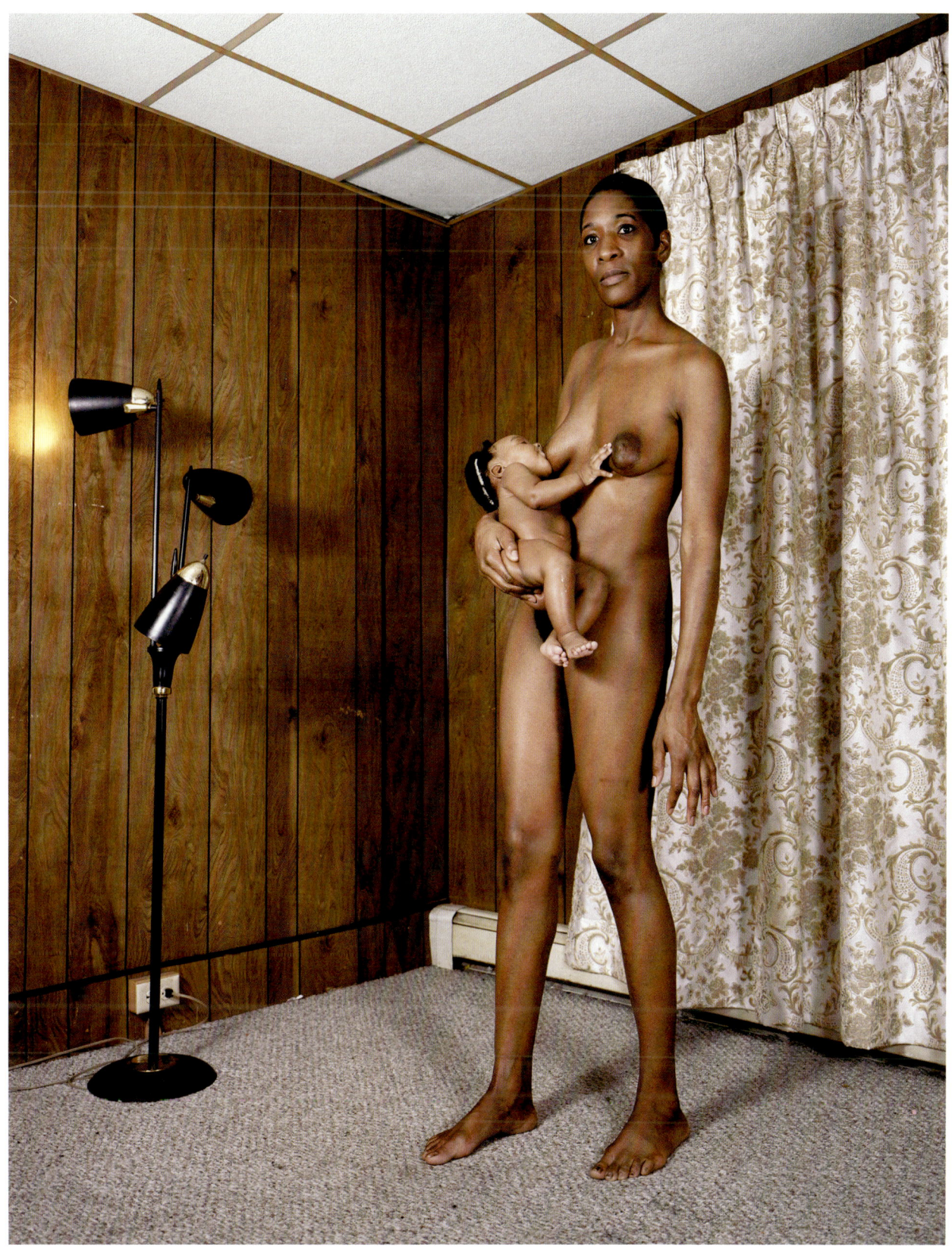

Mother and Child, Poughkeepsie, NY, 1999

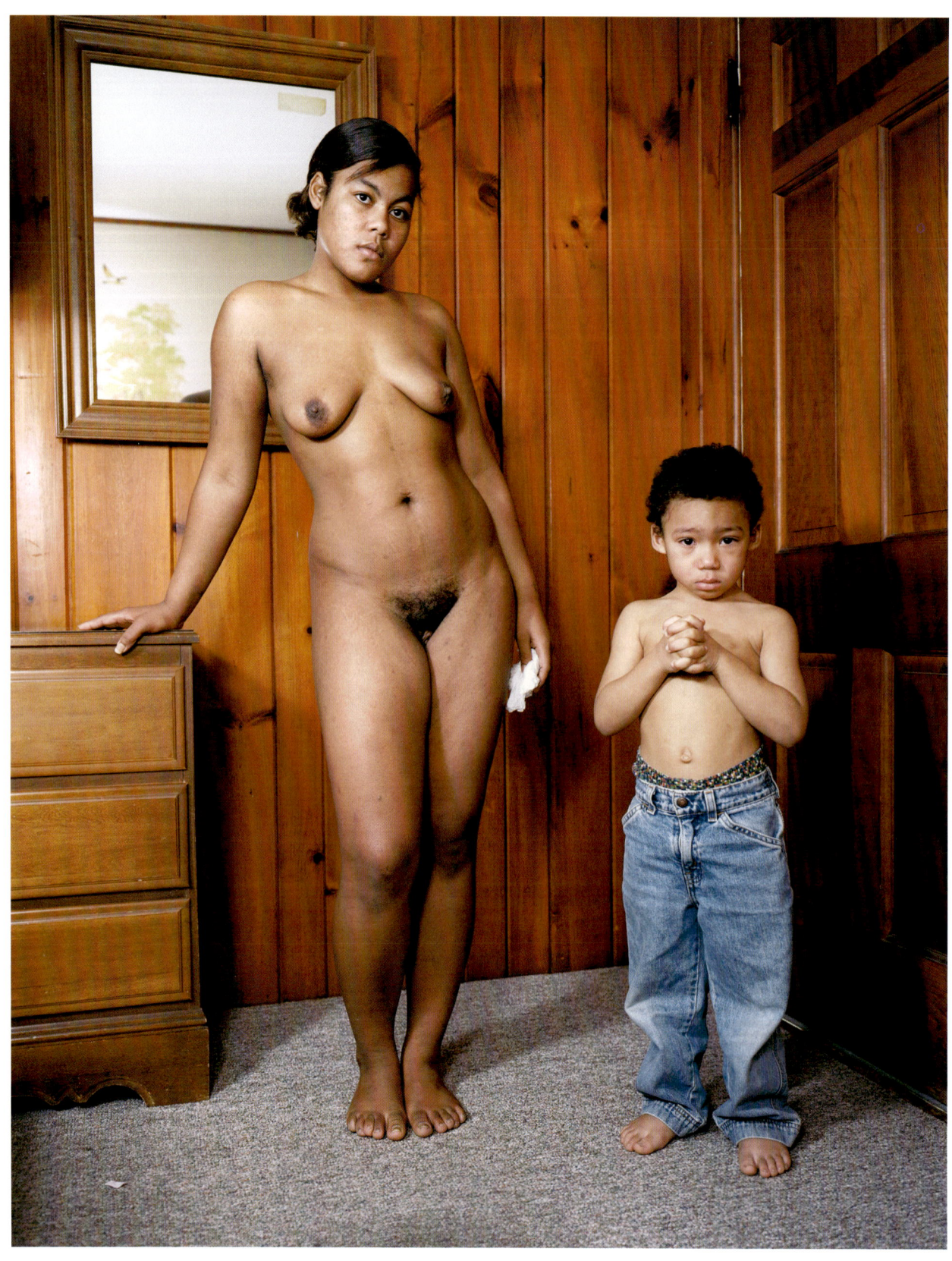

Mother and Son, Poughkeepsie, NY, 1999

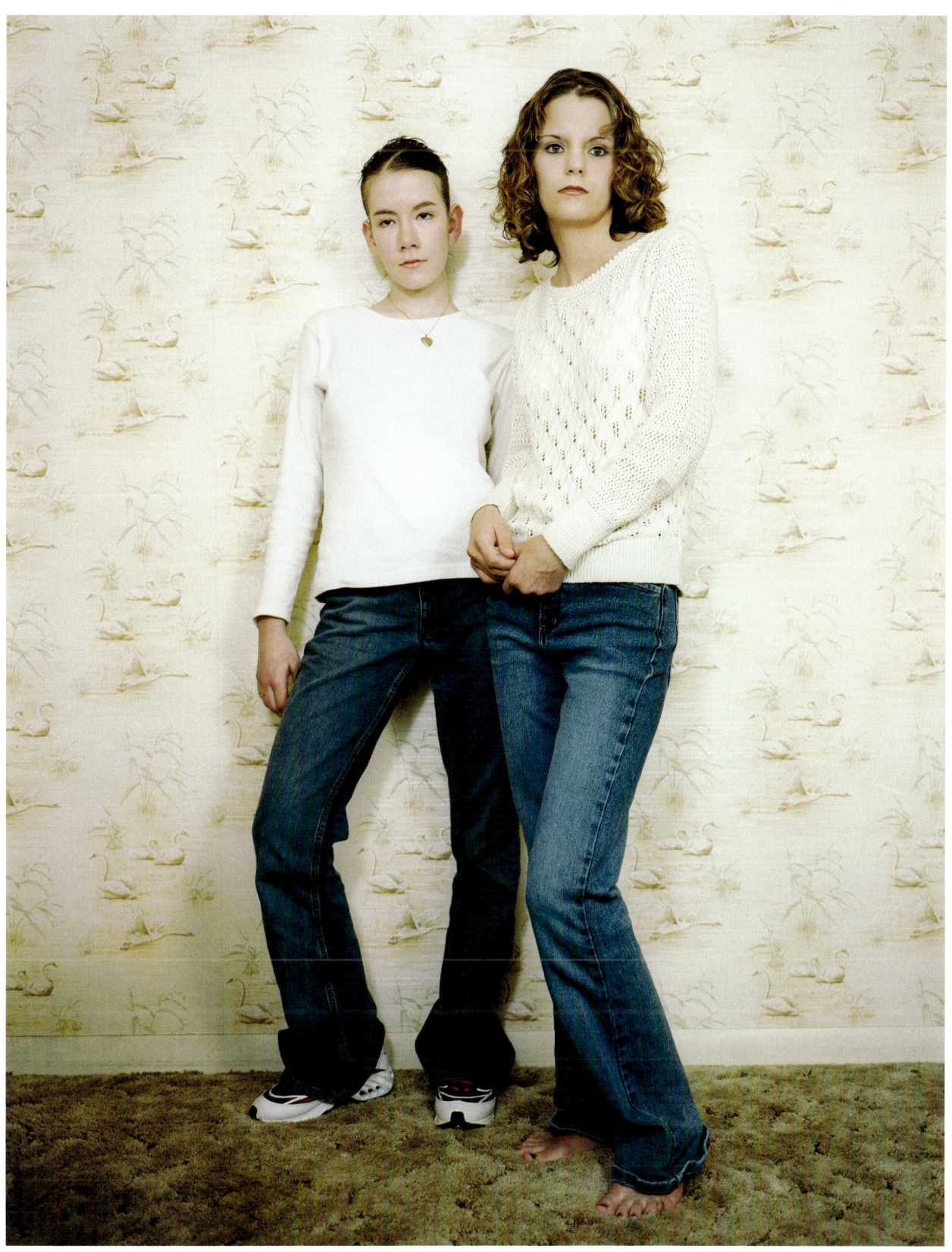

Young Mothers, Fitchberg, WI, 2000

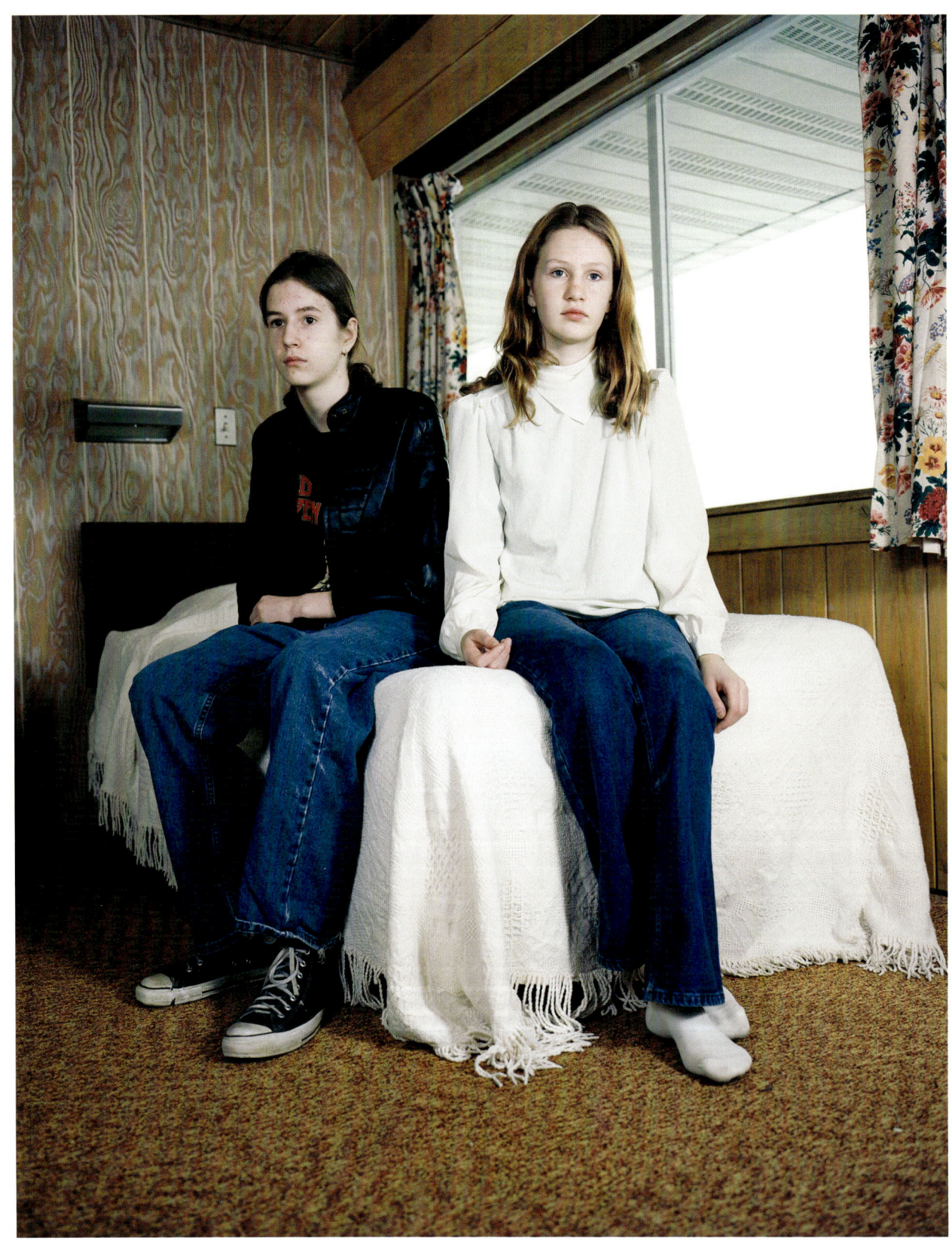

Brother and Sister, Red Hook, NY, 1999

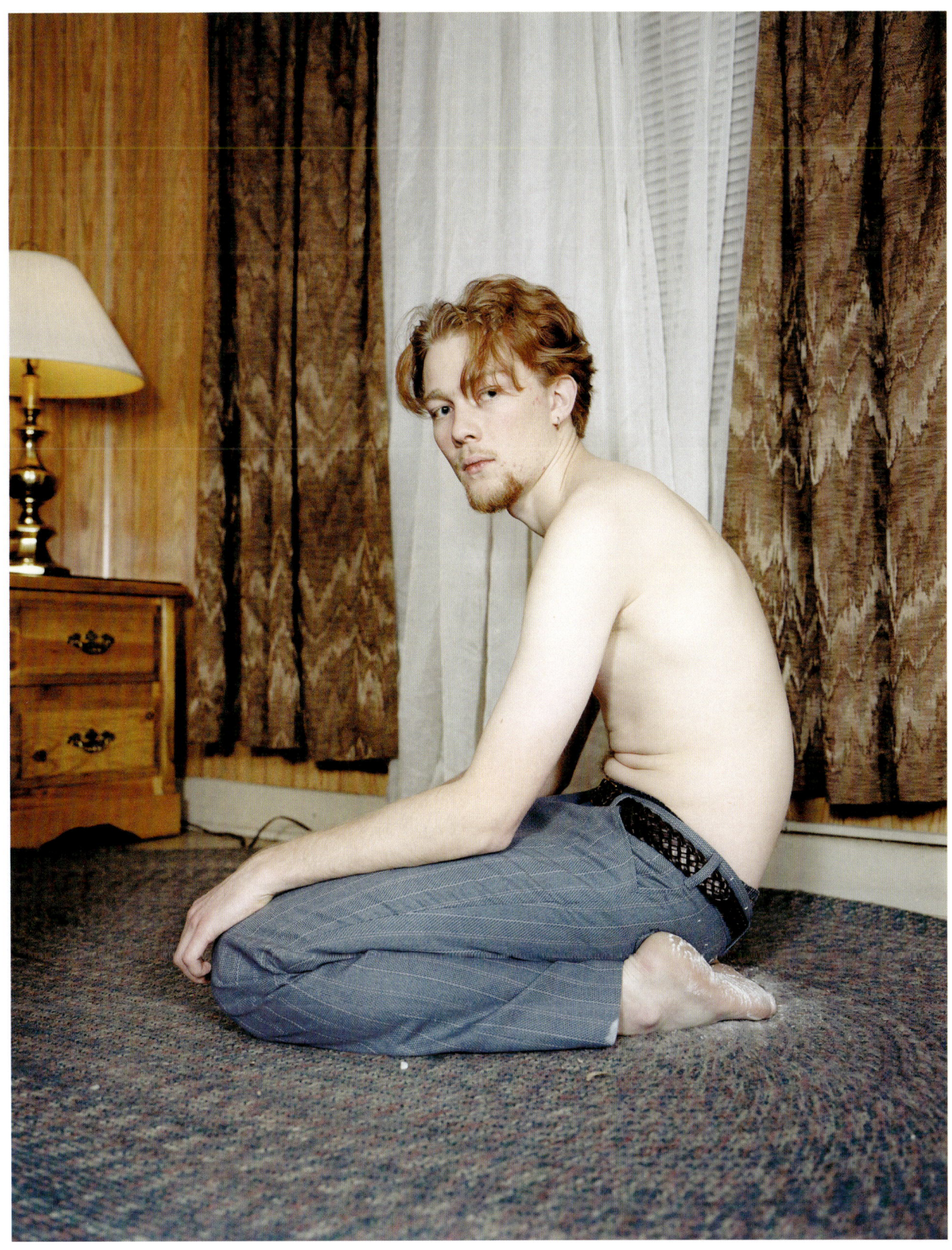

Wolf, Poughkeepsie, NY, 1999

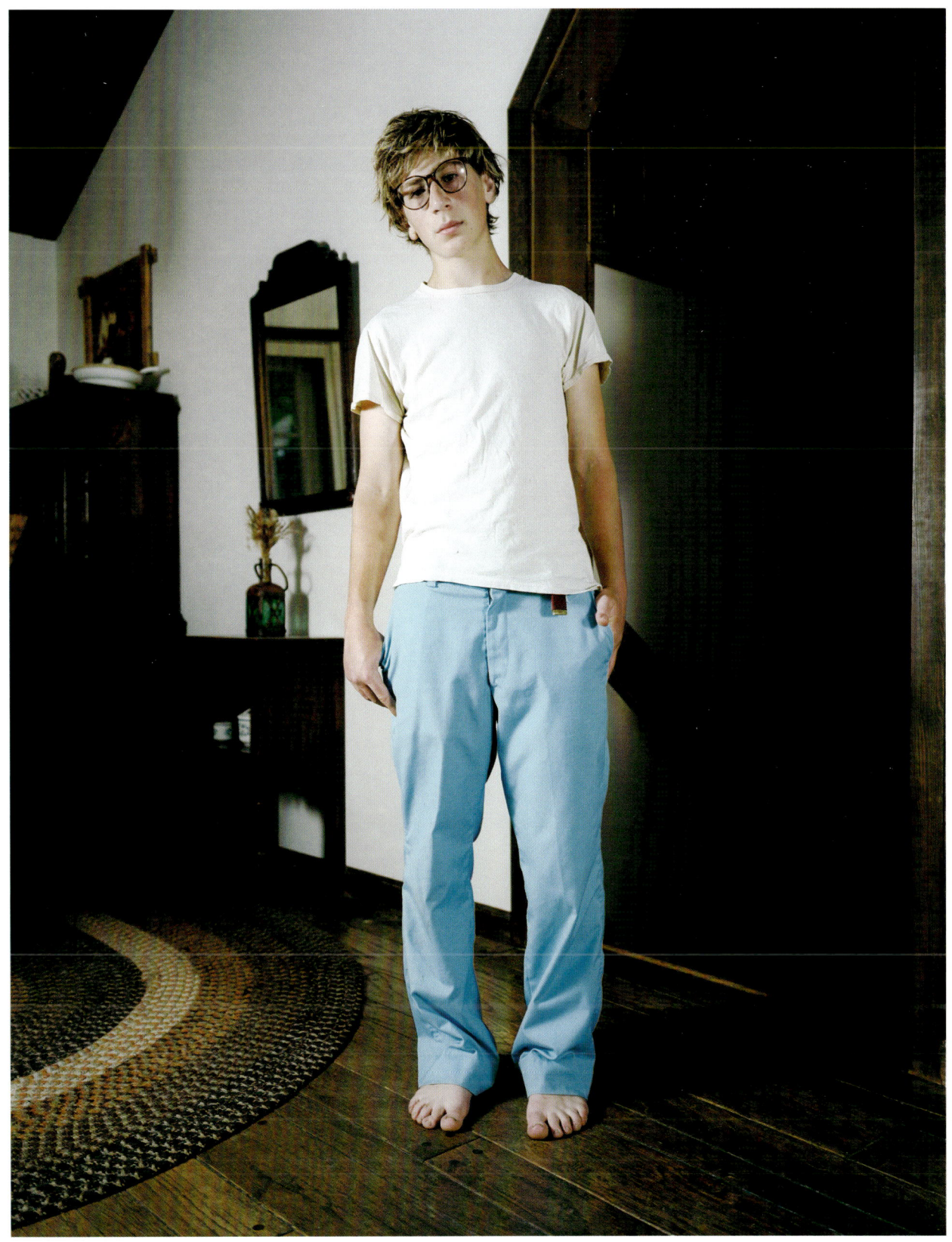

Rhinebeck, NY, 2000

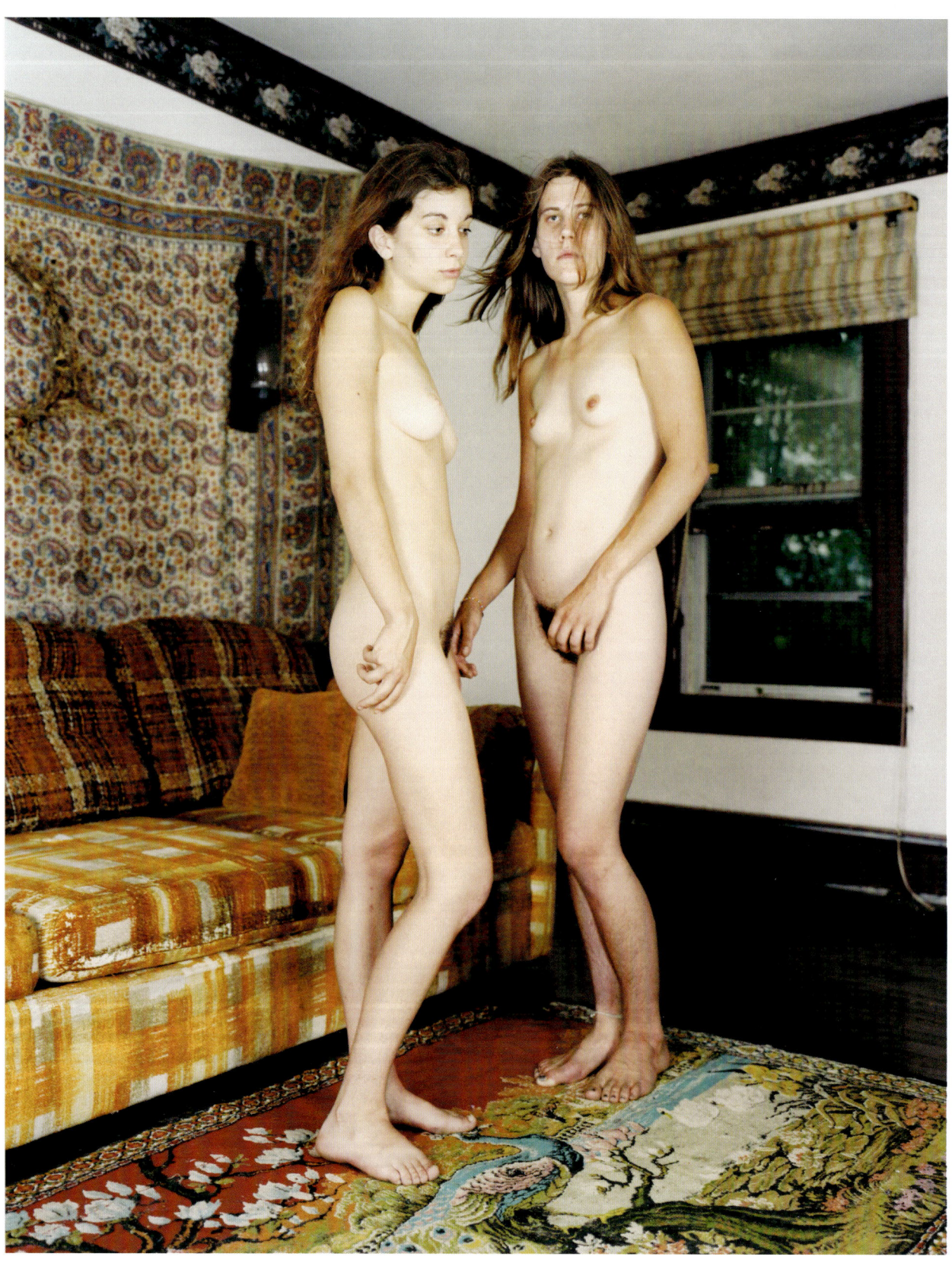

Friends, New Paltz, NY, 2000

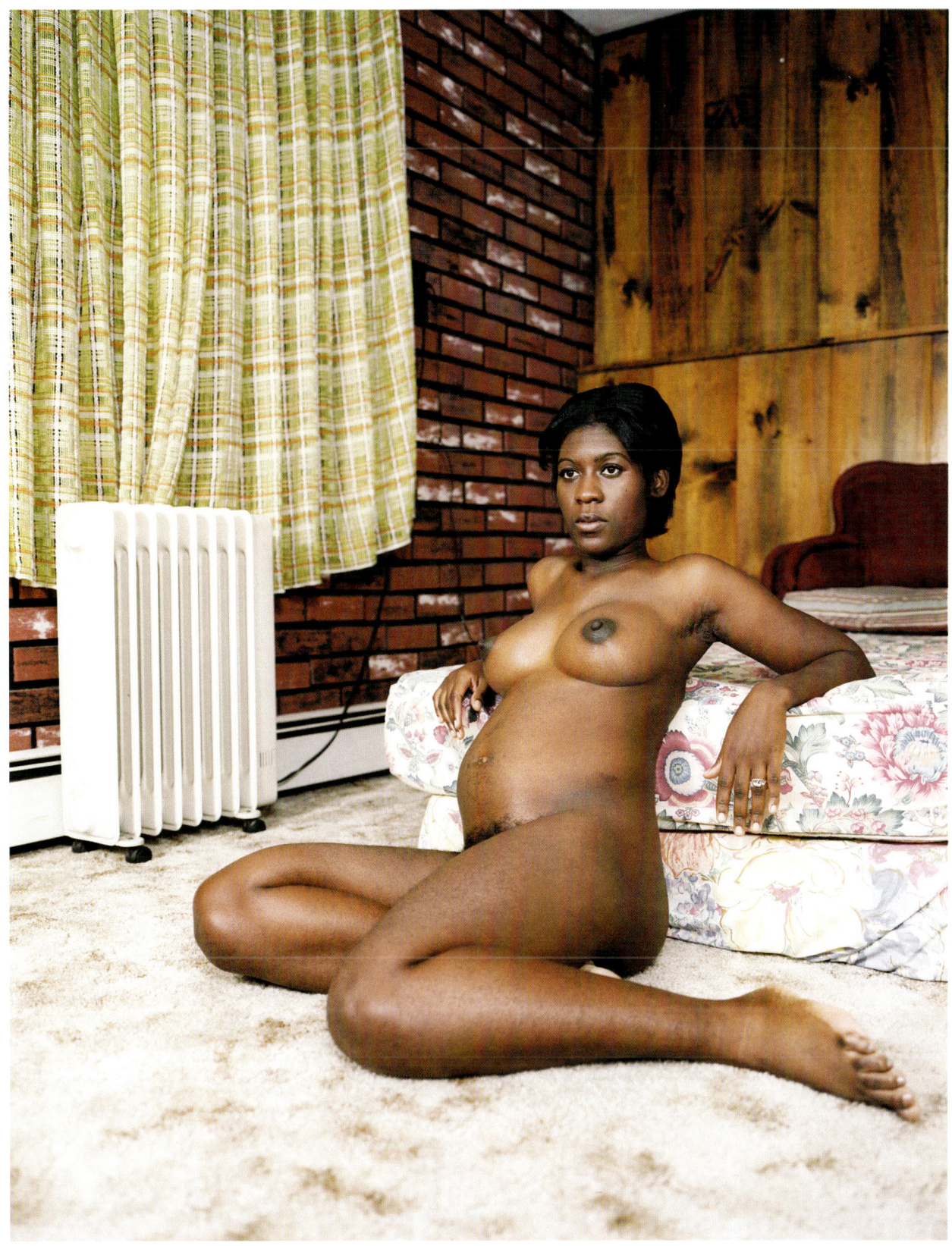

Hyde Park, NY, 1999

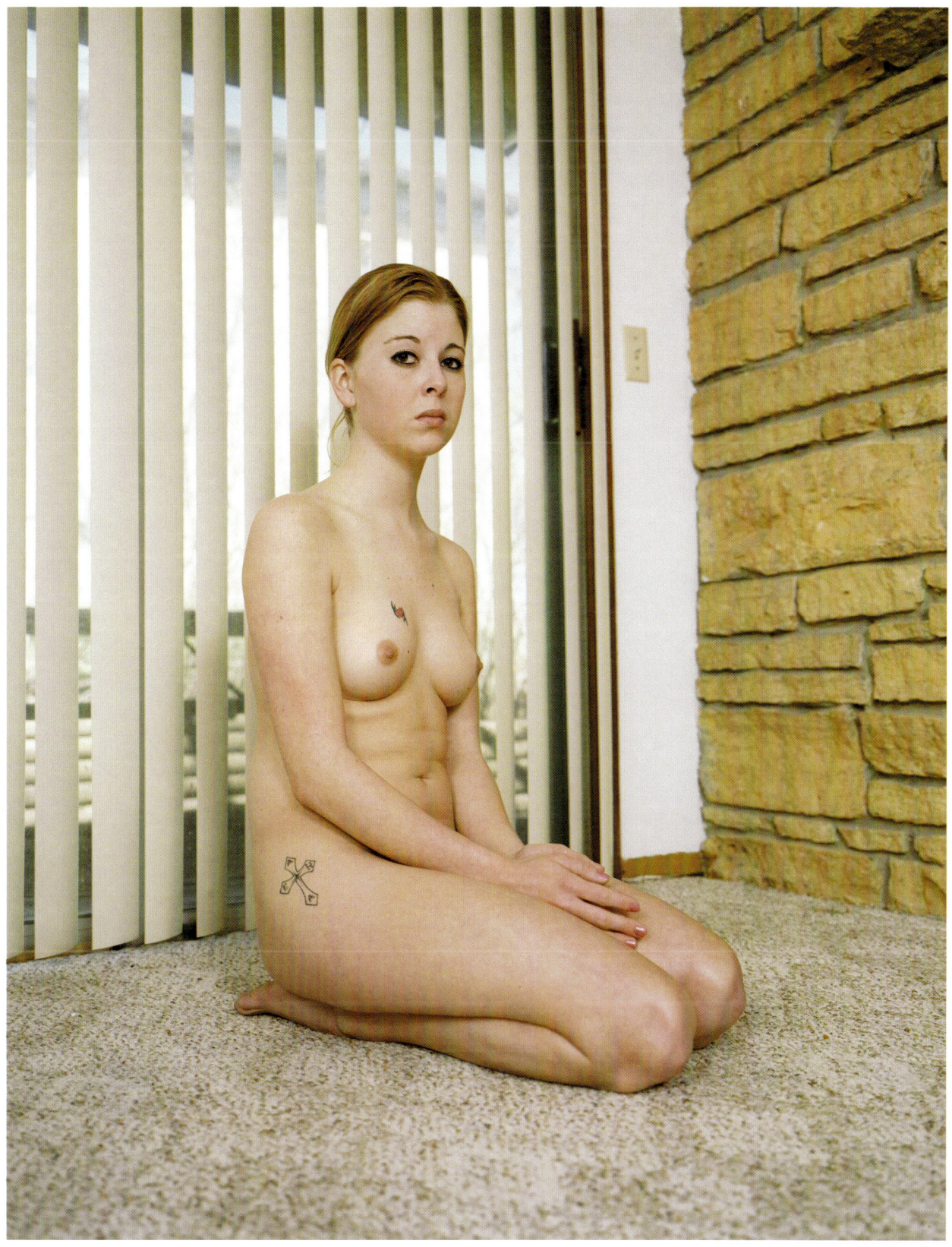

Middleton, WI, 2000

V. came back home to Ghent after her new friends in San Diego stole everything from her. She had moved out west the year before to become a rock star, she said, or a tattoo artist. She seemed upbeat though, and had just found a job at the 7-Eleven on Route 9. V. loved to be photographed. She curled up on the floor beneath the fish tank and the painting of waves crashing violently over rocks. It was just like being on a Pacific Coast beach, back before things went wrong.   **MORNING CALL**, 2001-2004

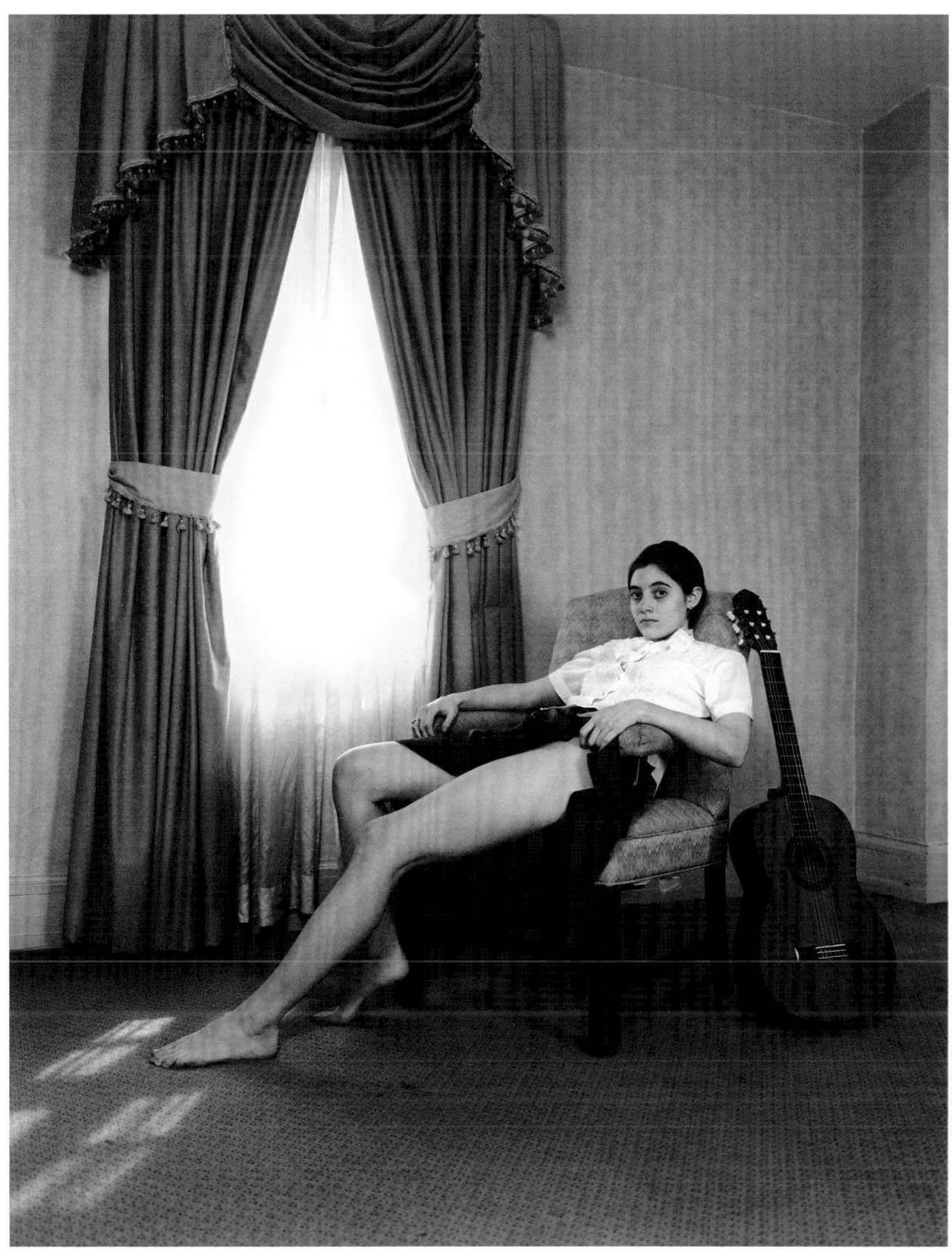

Deanna, Allentown, PA, 2001

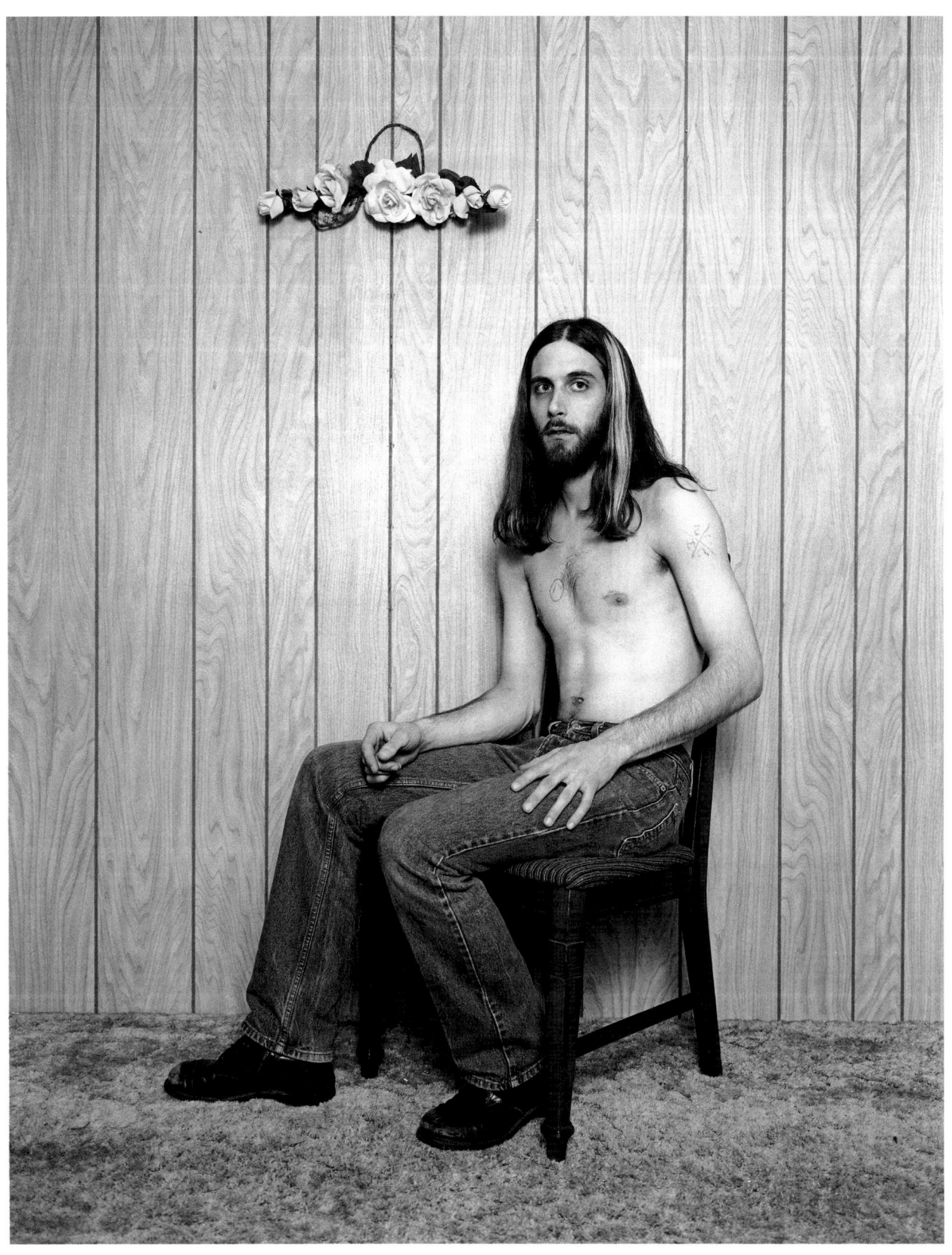

Barry, Bethlehem, PA, 2002

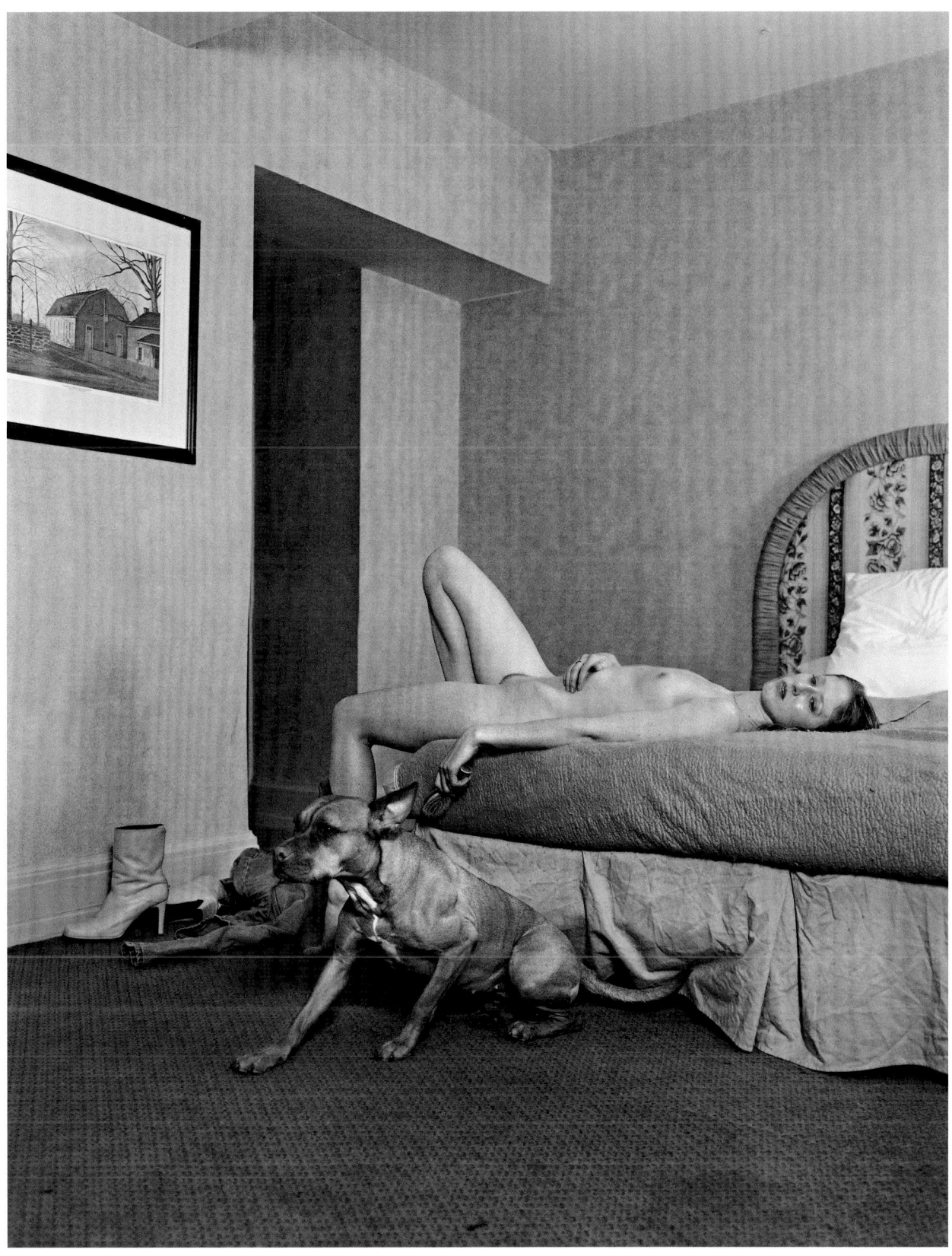

Angie and Betty, Allentown, PA, 2002

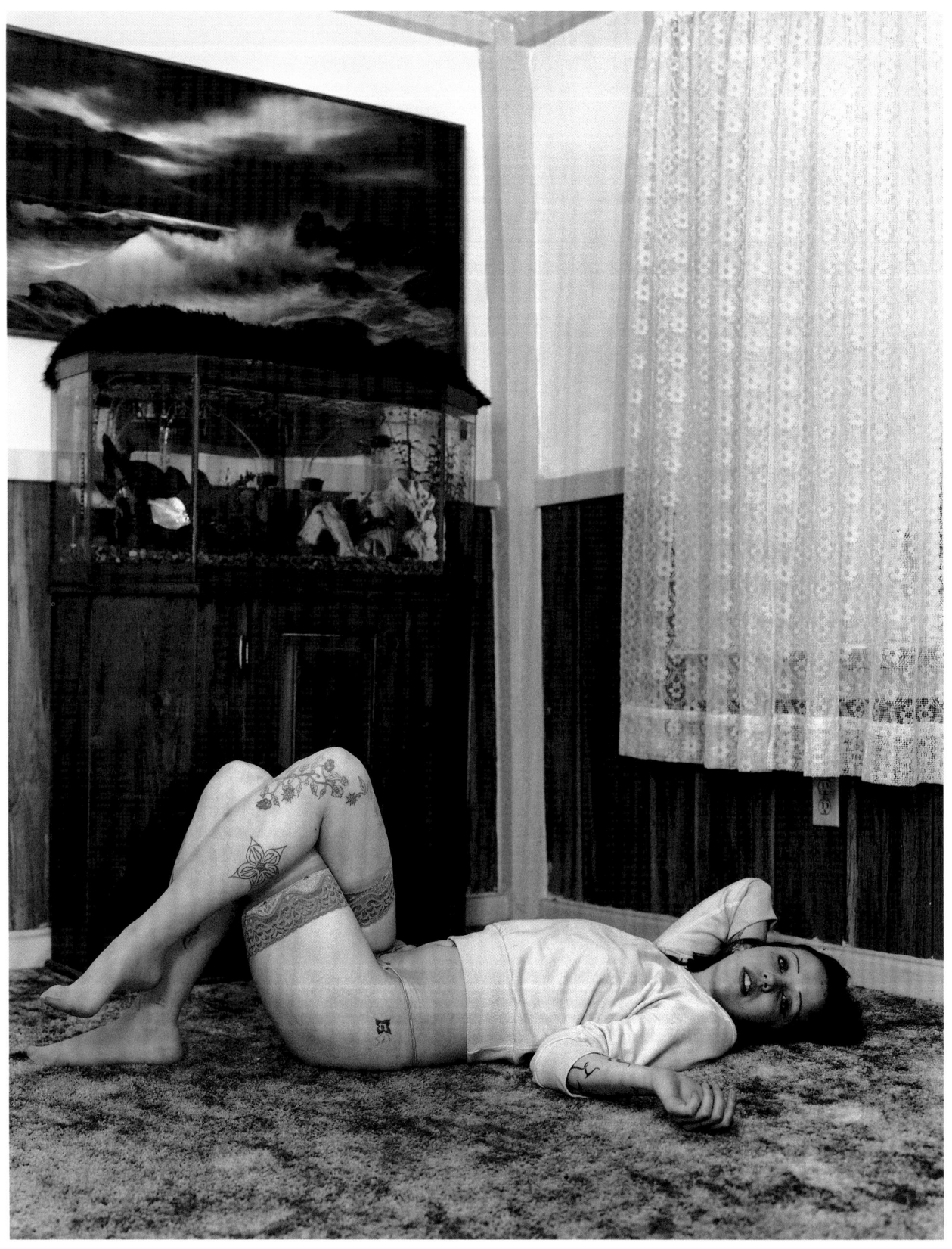

Valerie, Valatie, NY, 2003

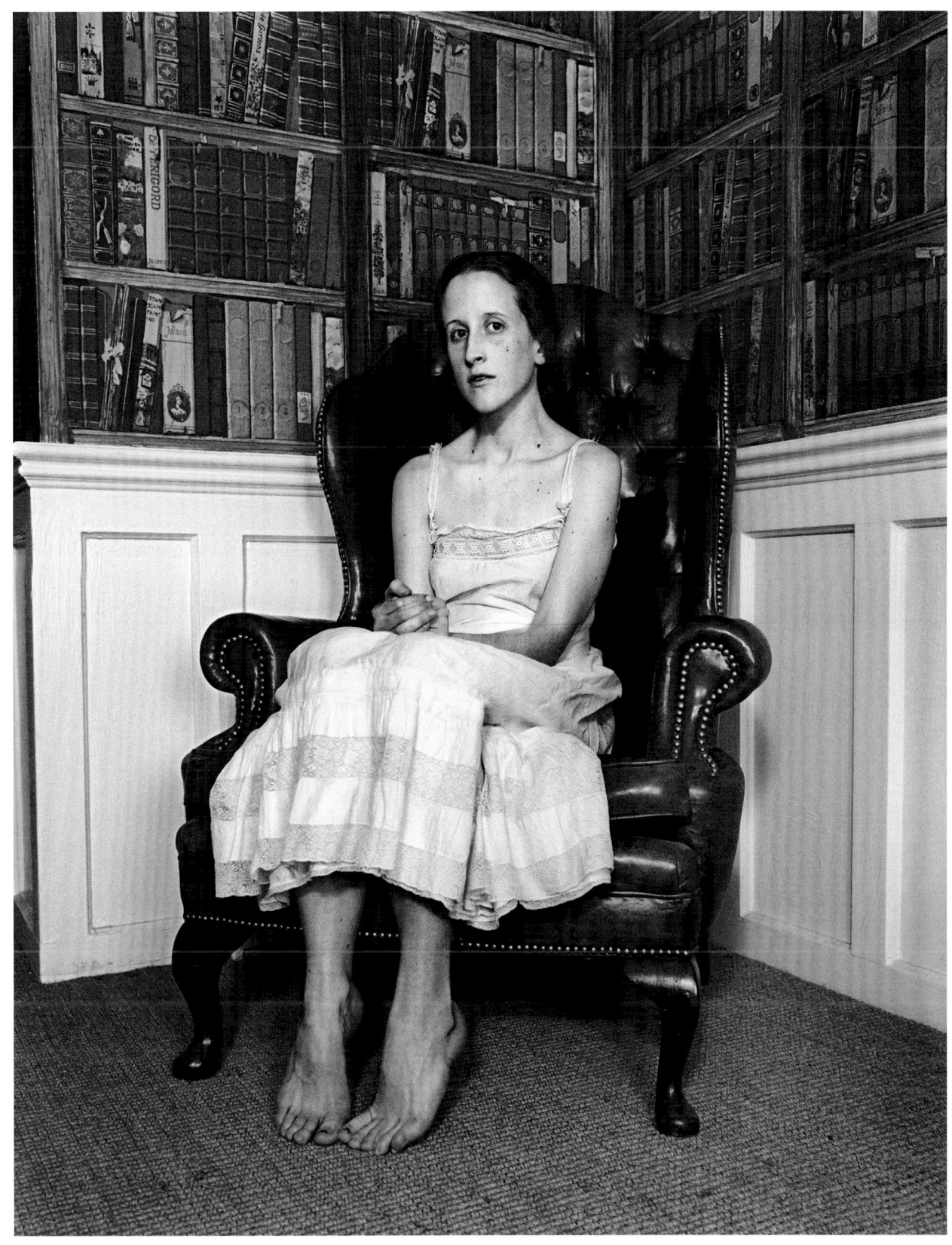

Corinne, New York, NY, 2001

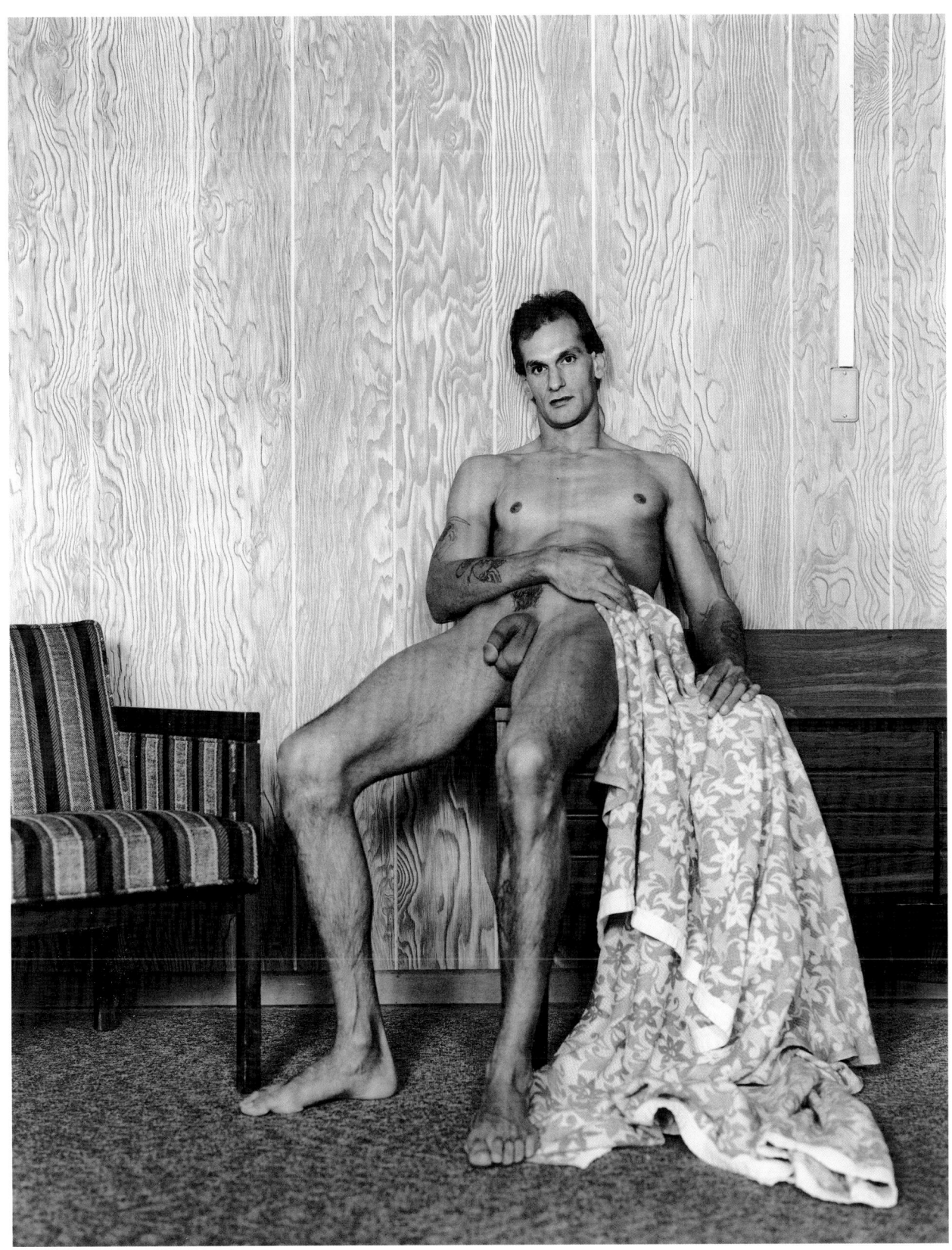

Mike, Hearthstone Motel, Upper Red Hook, NY, 2004

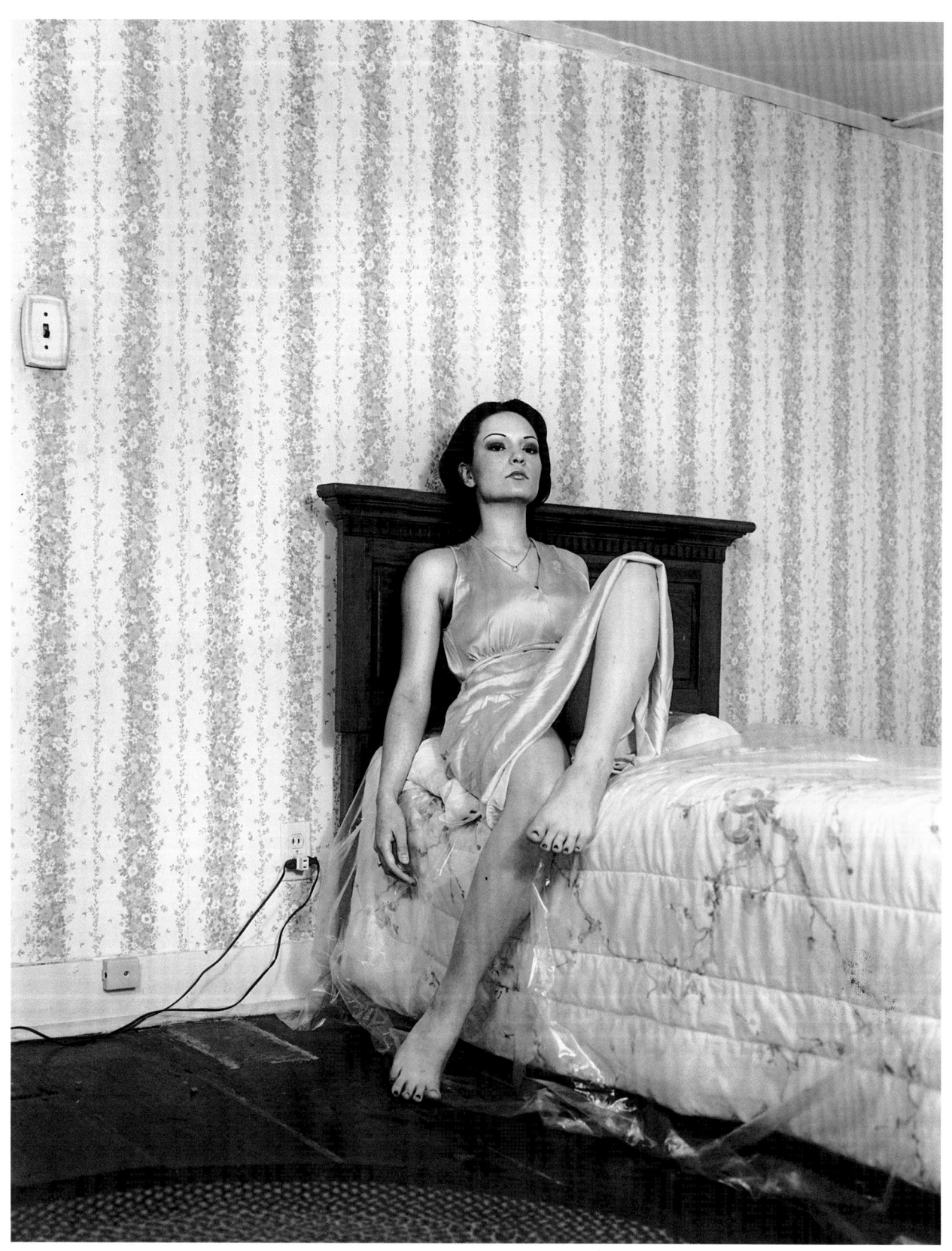

Maribeth, Grandmother's House, Poughkeepsie, NY, 2003

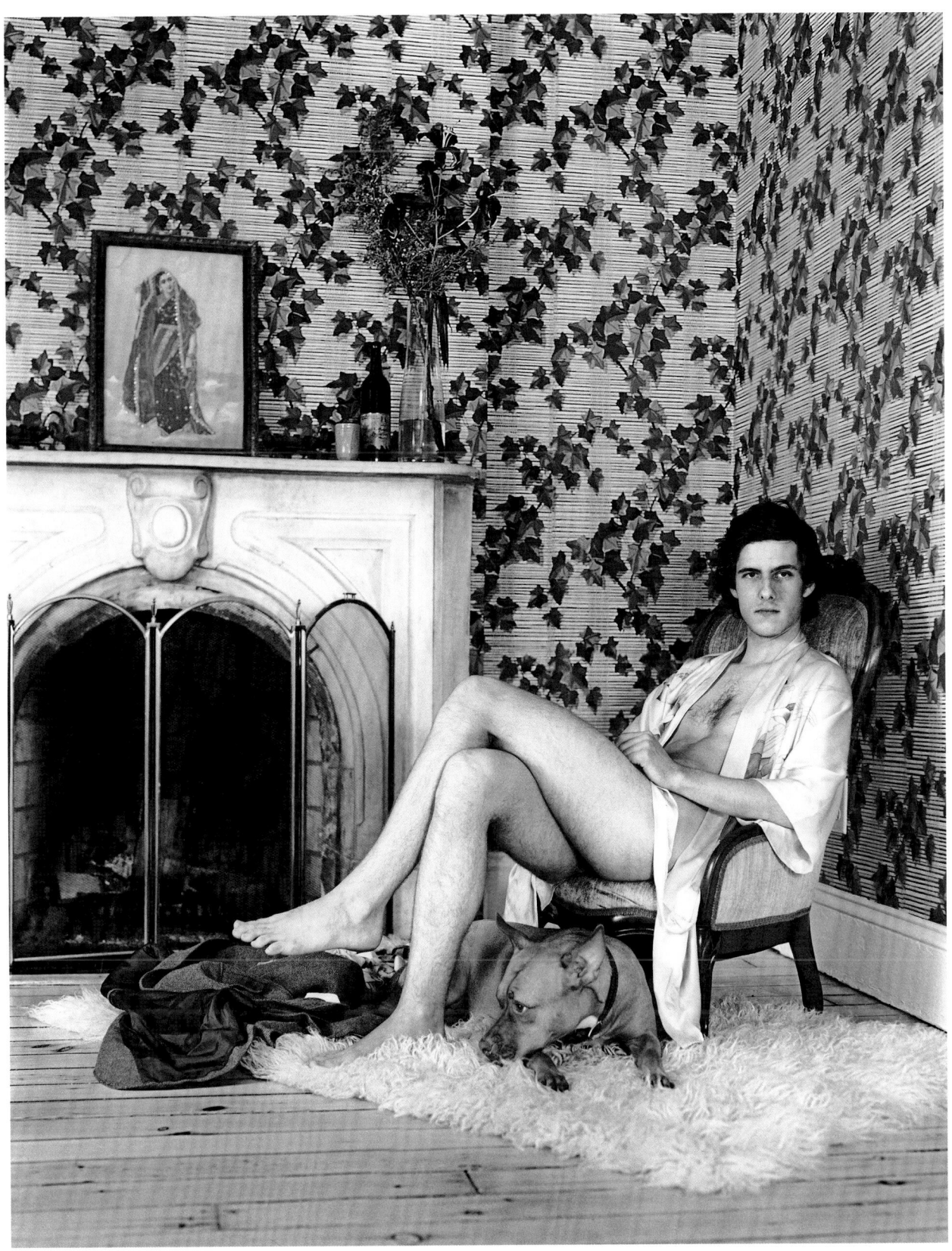

Van, Red Hook, Brooklyn, NY, 2003

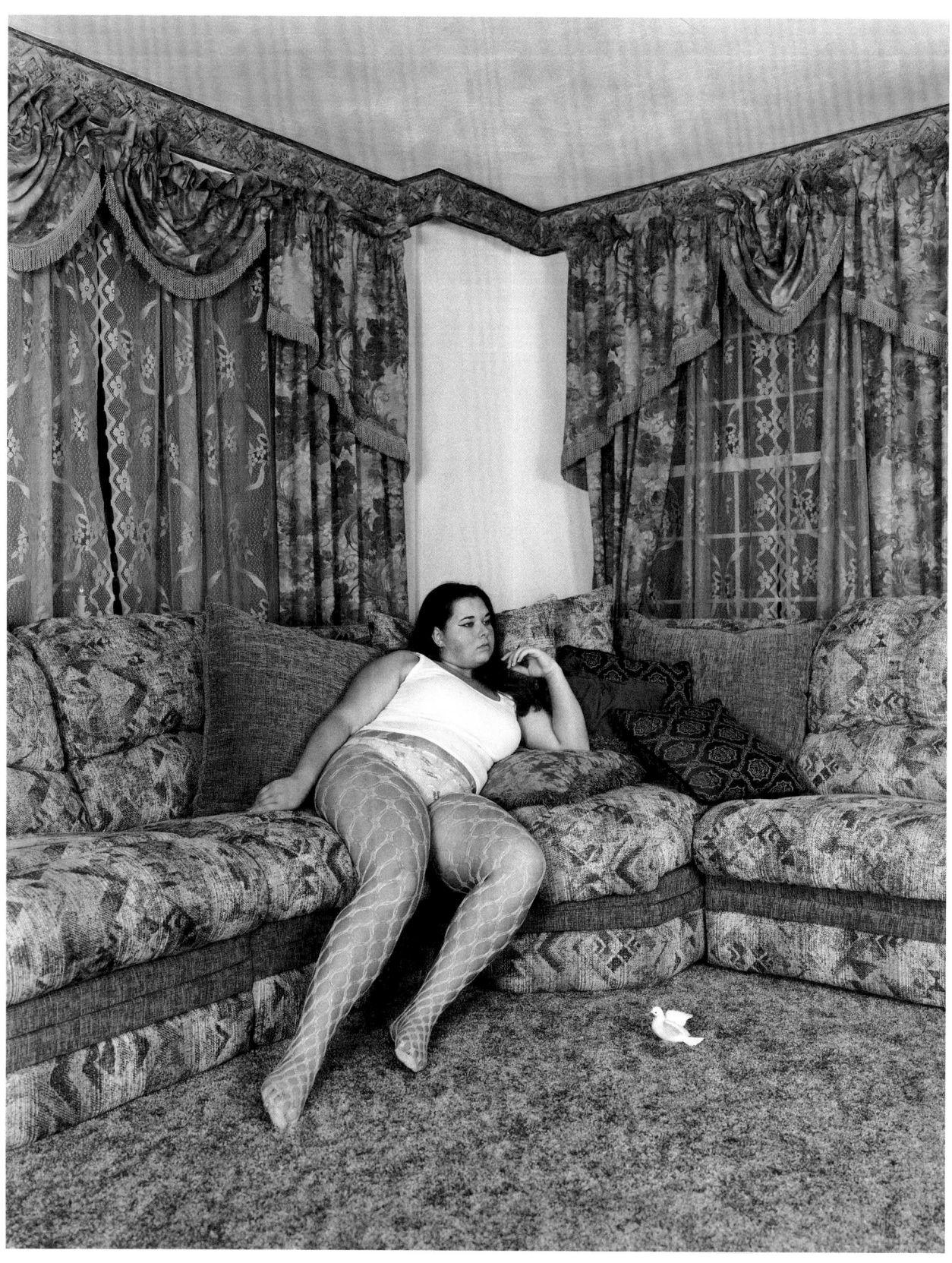

Joline, Broad Top, PA, 2002

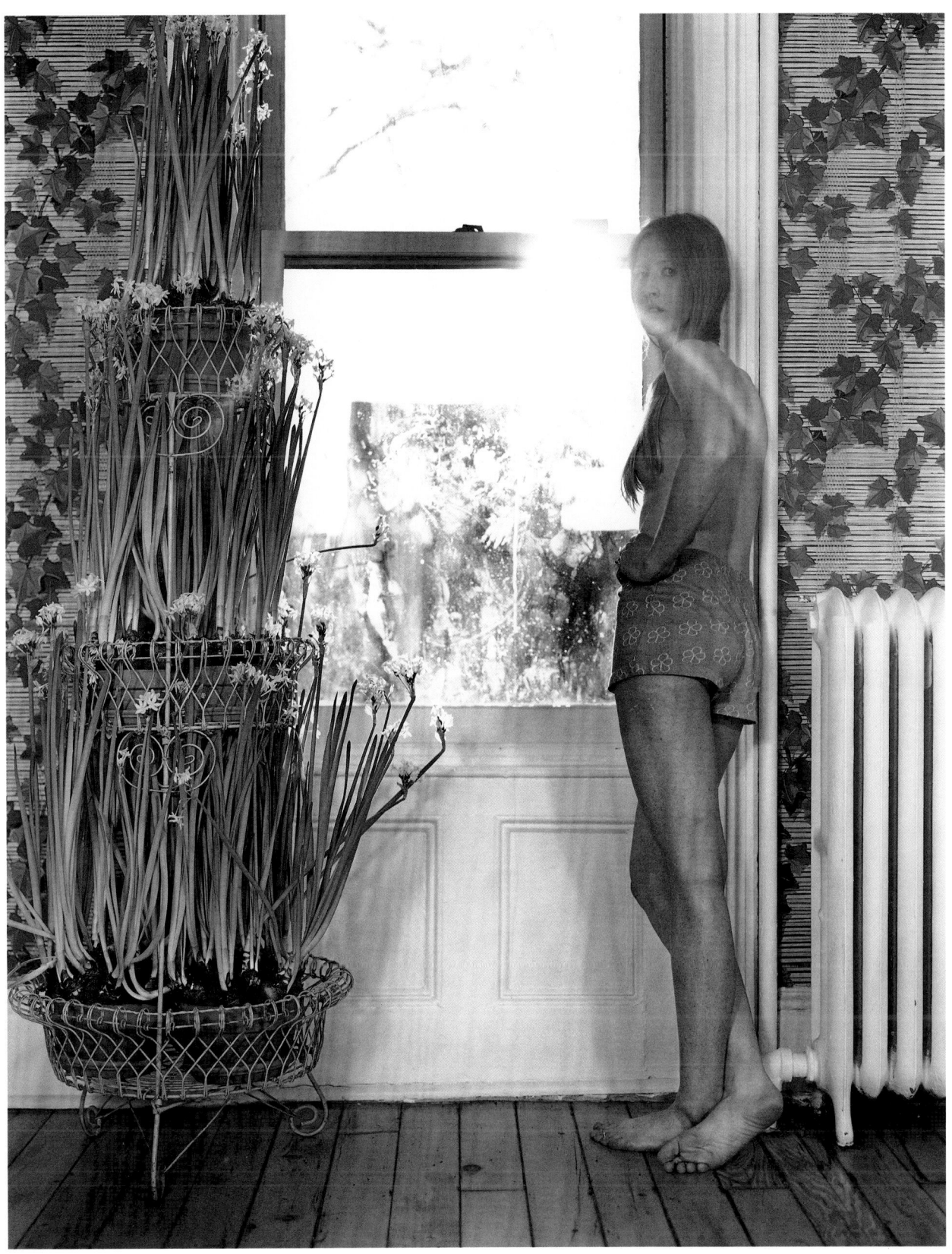

Angela, Red Hook, Brooklyn, NY, 2003

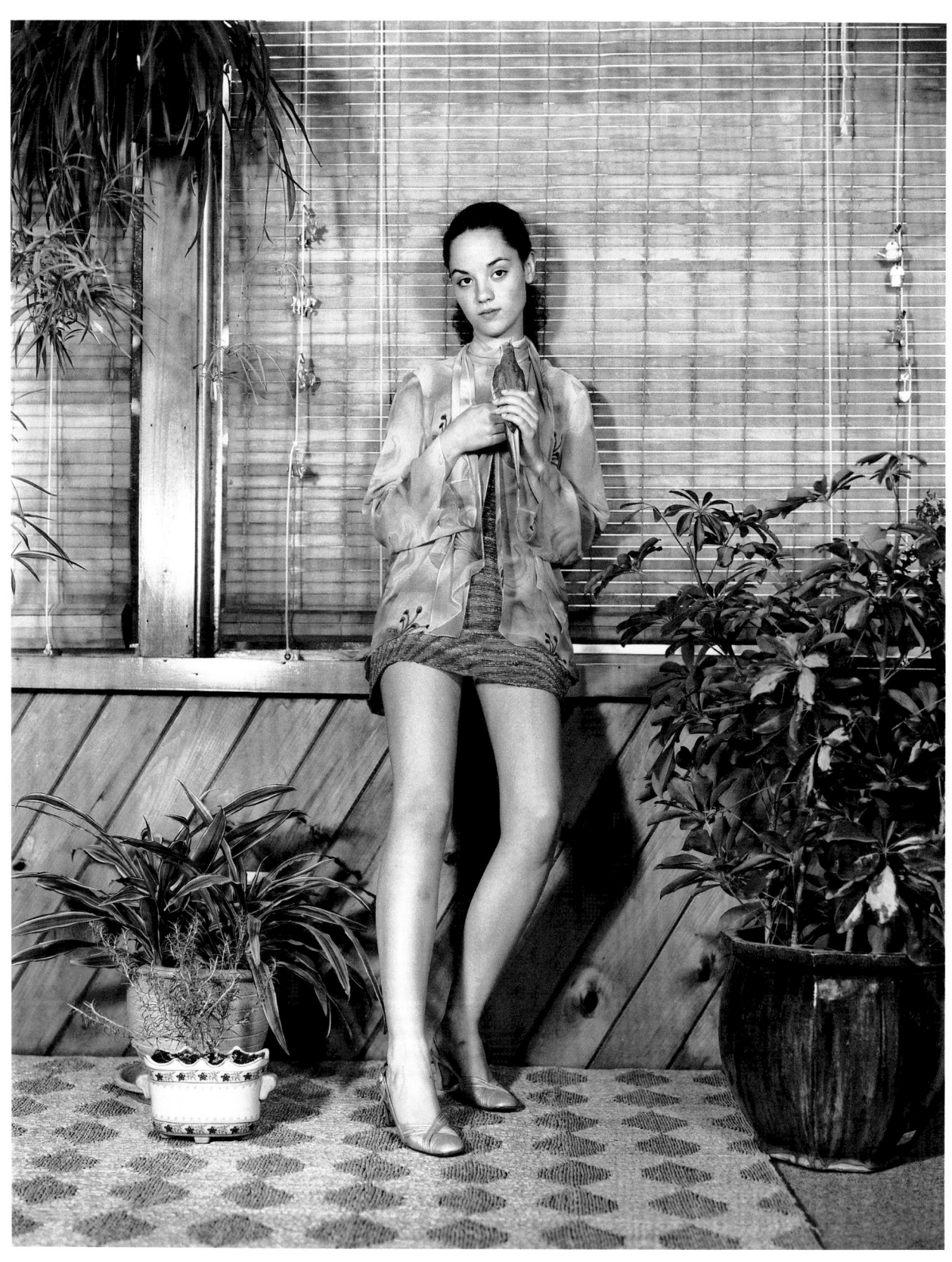

Taryn and Bird, Pinardville, NH, 2003

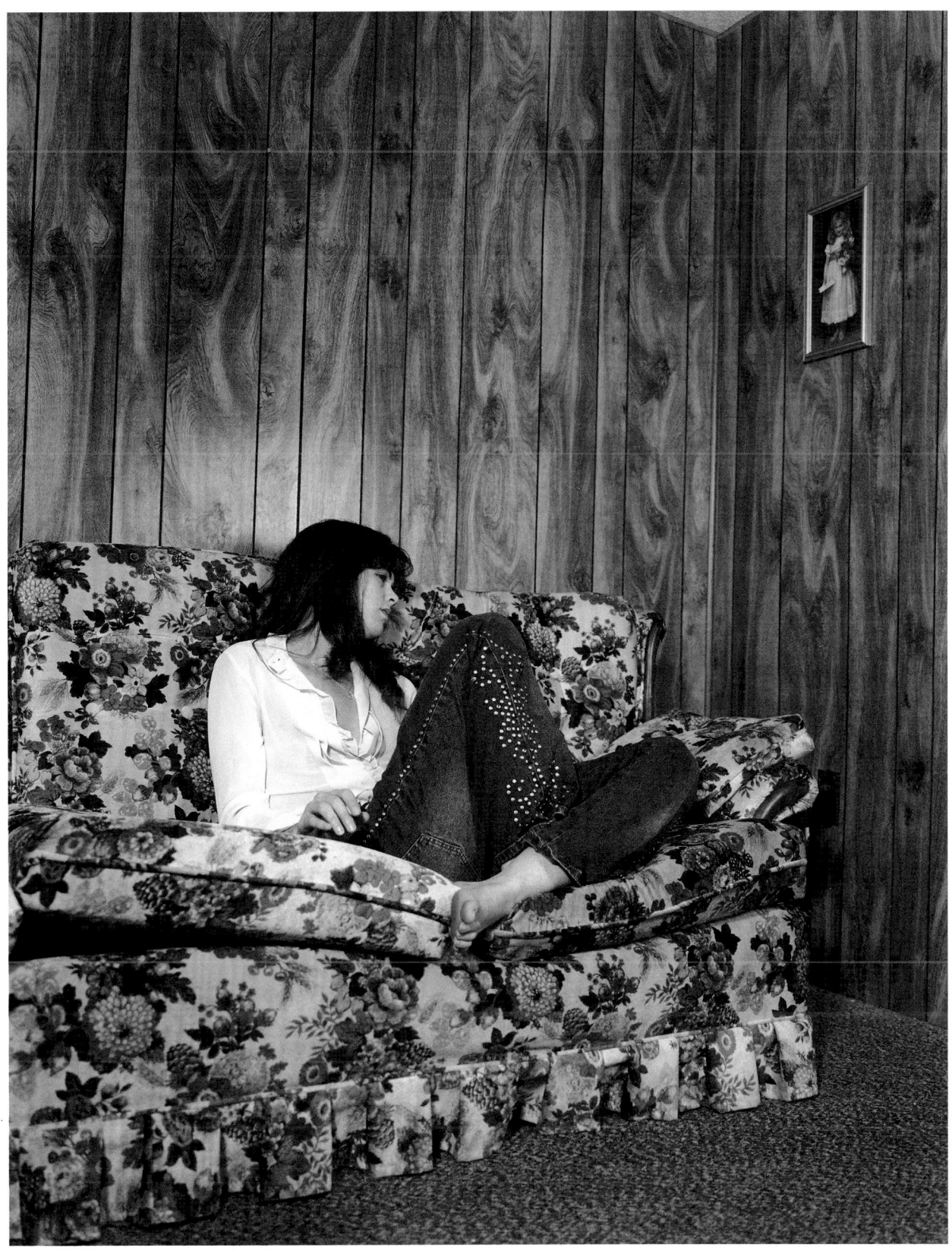

Jennifer, Easton, PA, 2001

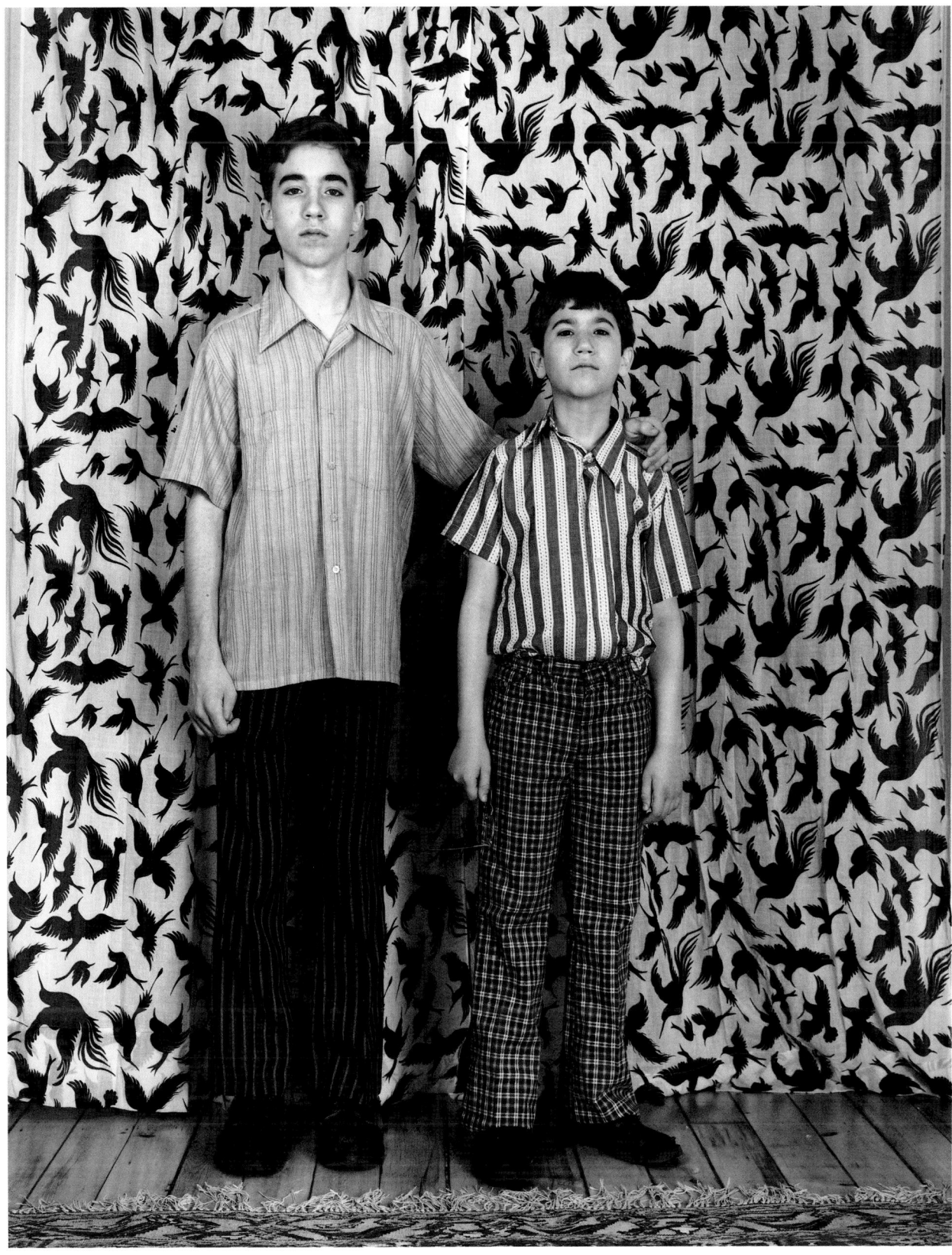

Michael and Evan, Red Hook, Brooklyn, NY, 2003

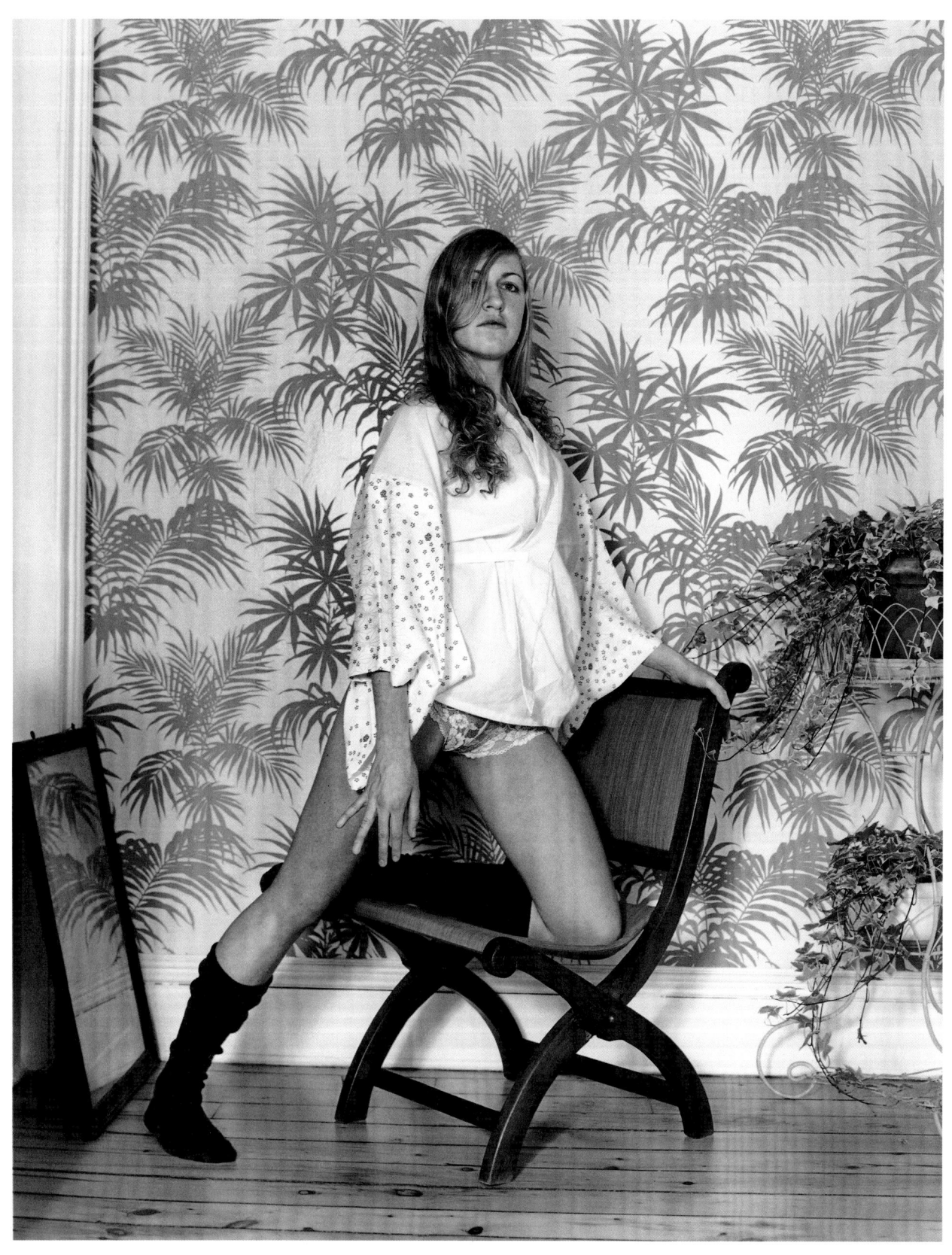

Diana, Red Hook, Brooklyn, NY, 2003

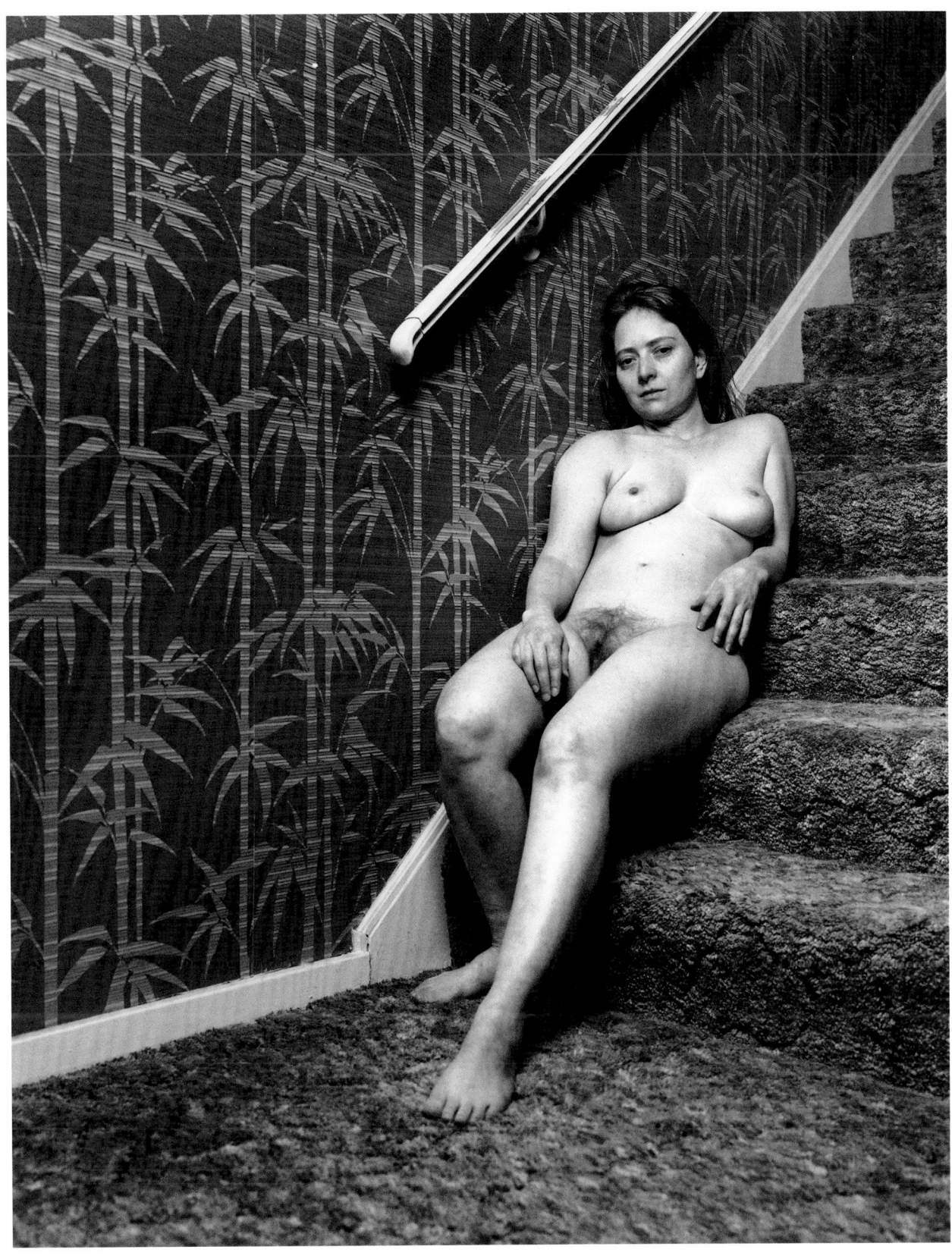

Christina, Allentown, PA, 2002

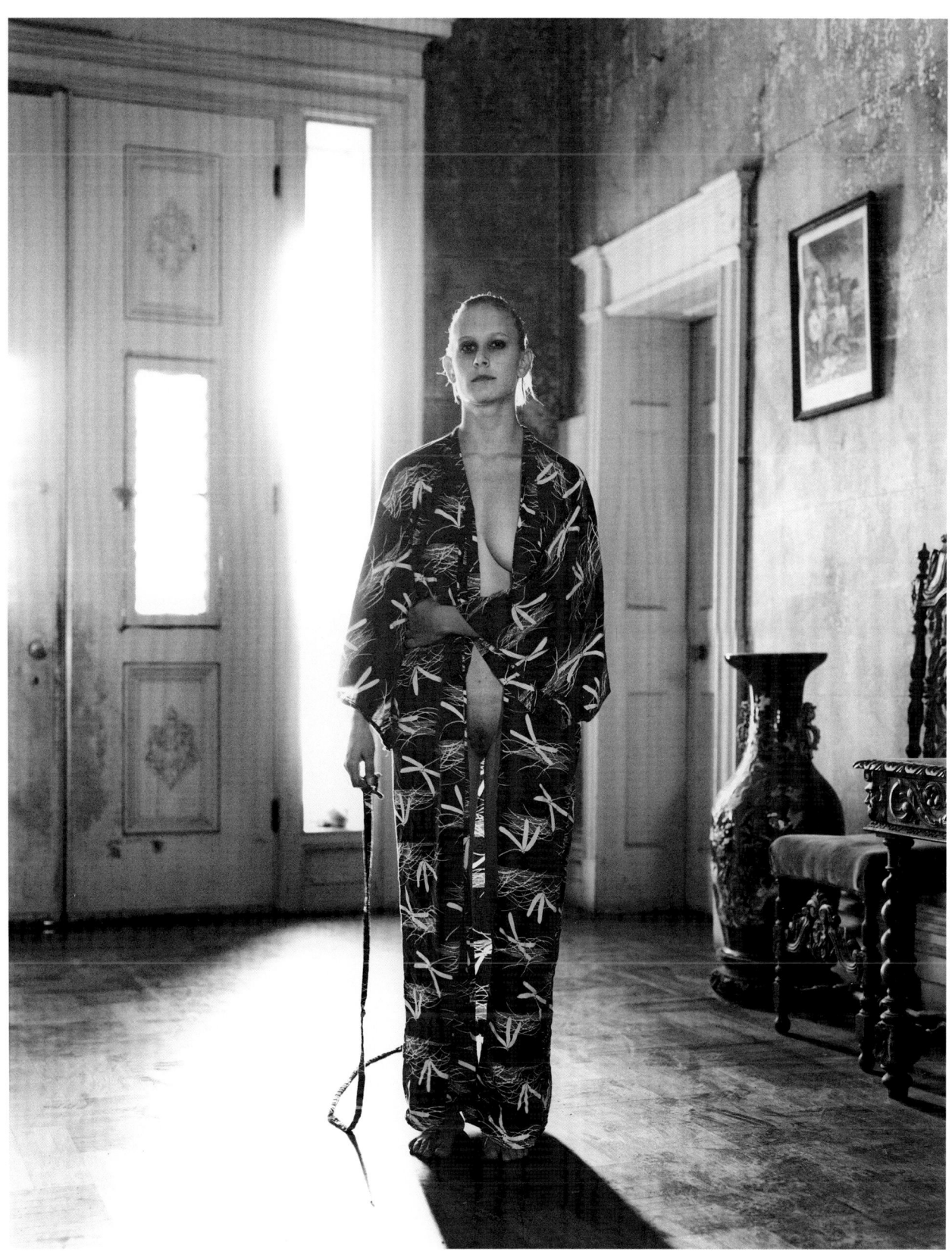

Alexis, Rokabe Farm, Rhinebeck, NY, 2003

M. asked me to hang up if his wife answered the phone. He said she wouldn't understand. We met twice. Once trespassing on someone's property in New Paltz and later at the Hearthstone Motel in Red Hook. M. was tall and lean with a graceful, almost feminine body. He stretched out on the blue towel he brought to protect himself from the ground. **SUGAR CAMP ROAD**, 2002-2003

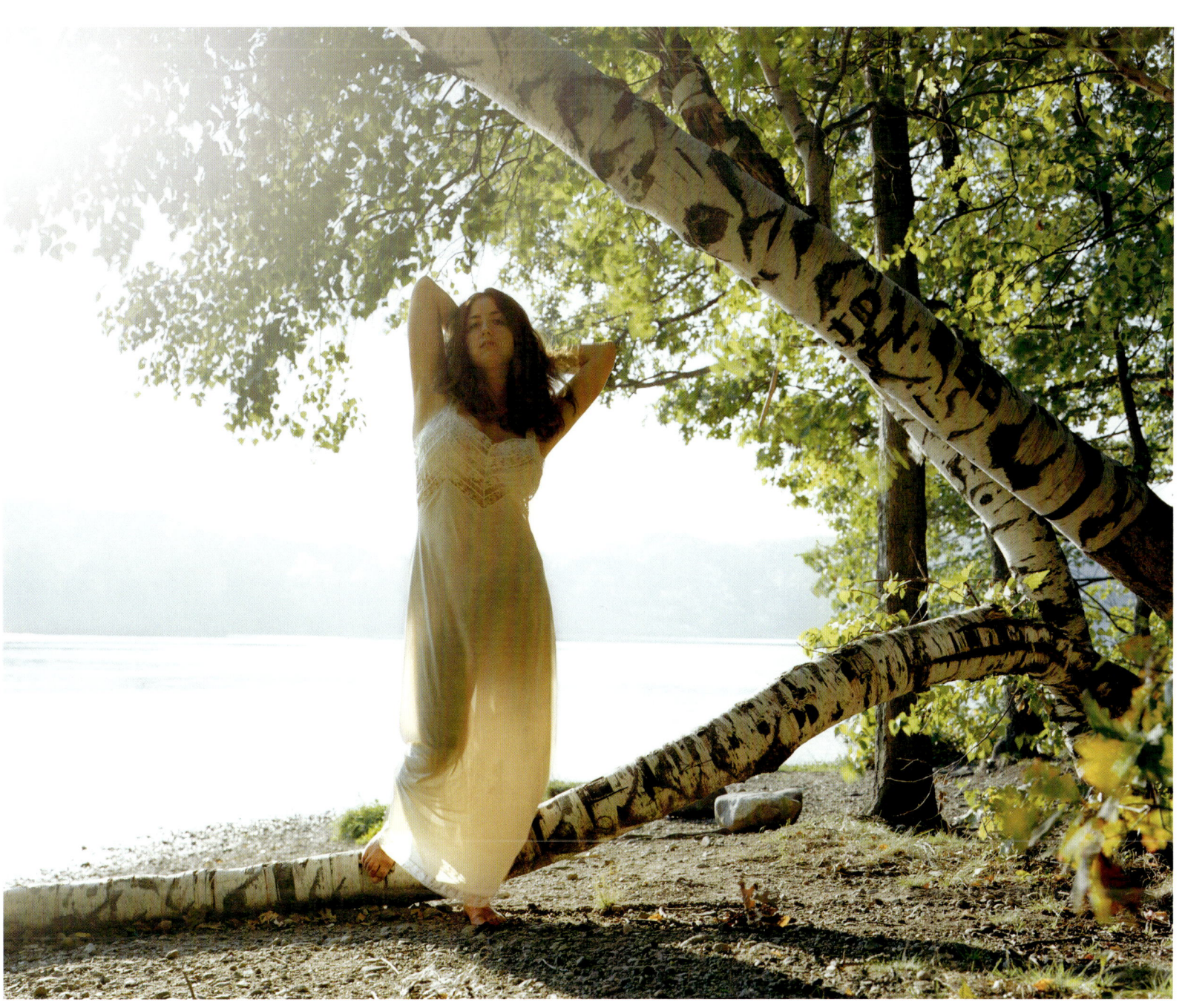

Joshi, Mystic Lake, MA, 2002

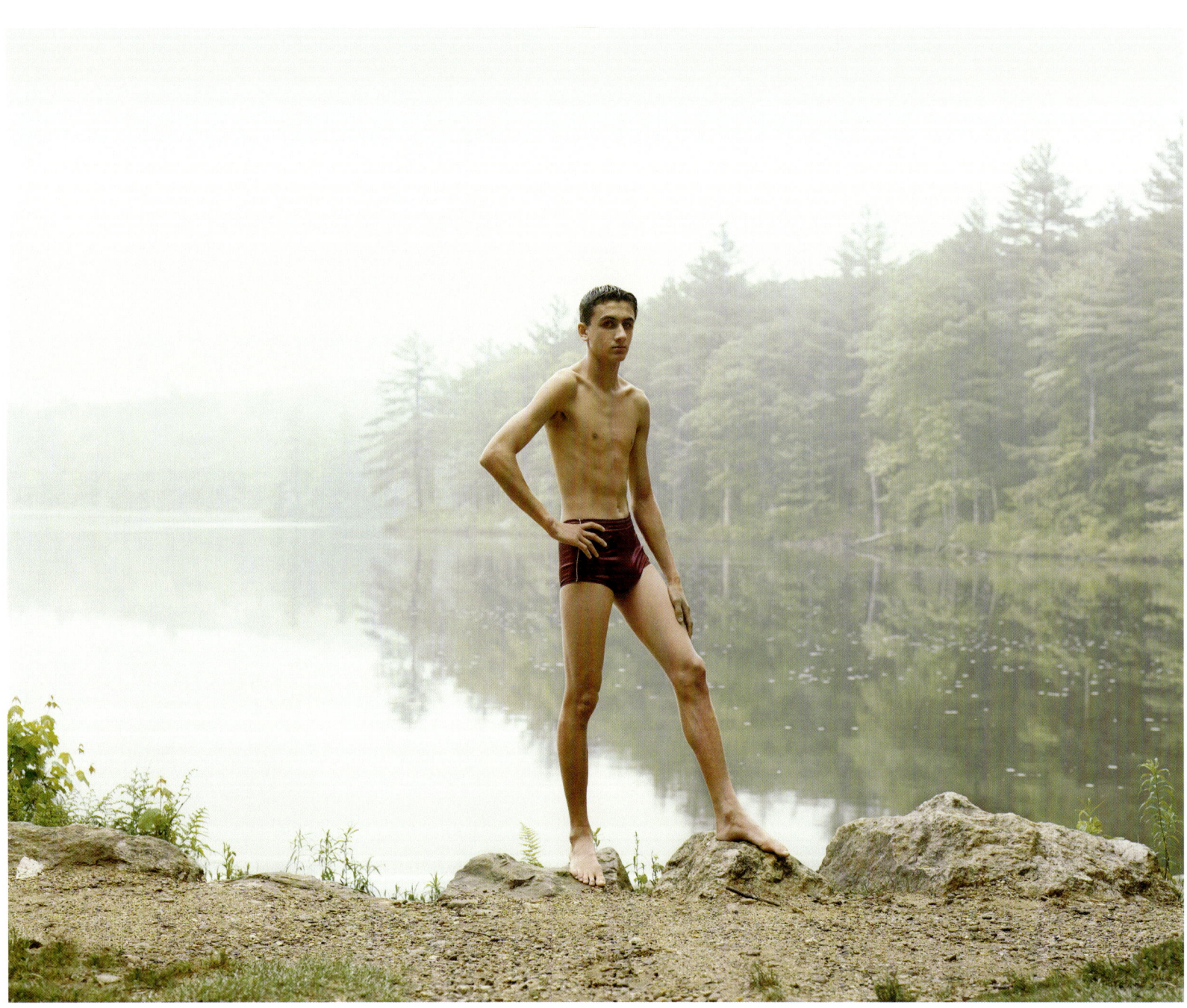

Corey, Quabbin Reservoir, Barre, MA, 2003

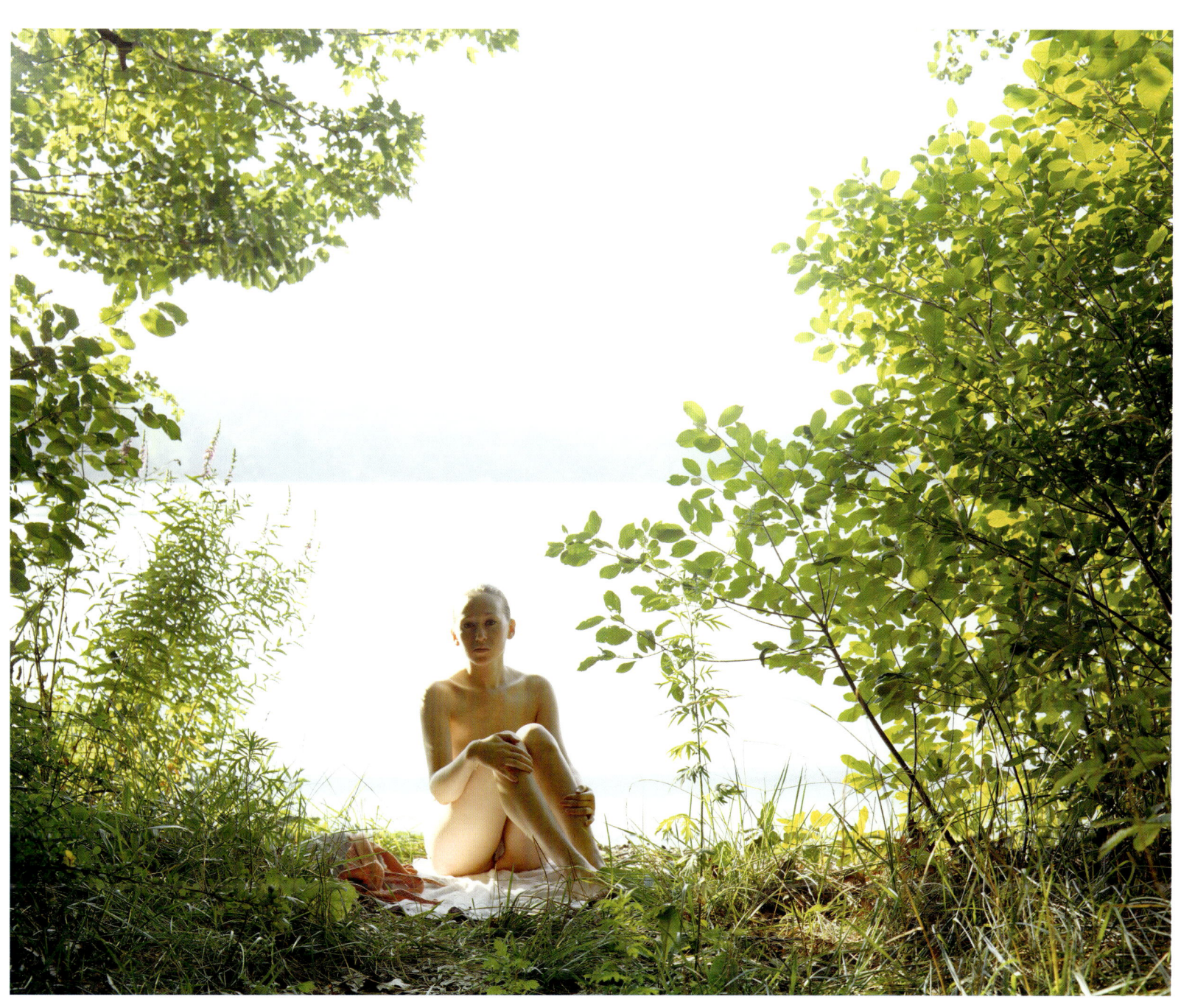

Shana, Mystic Lake, Medford, MA, 2002

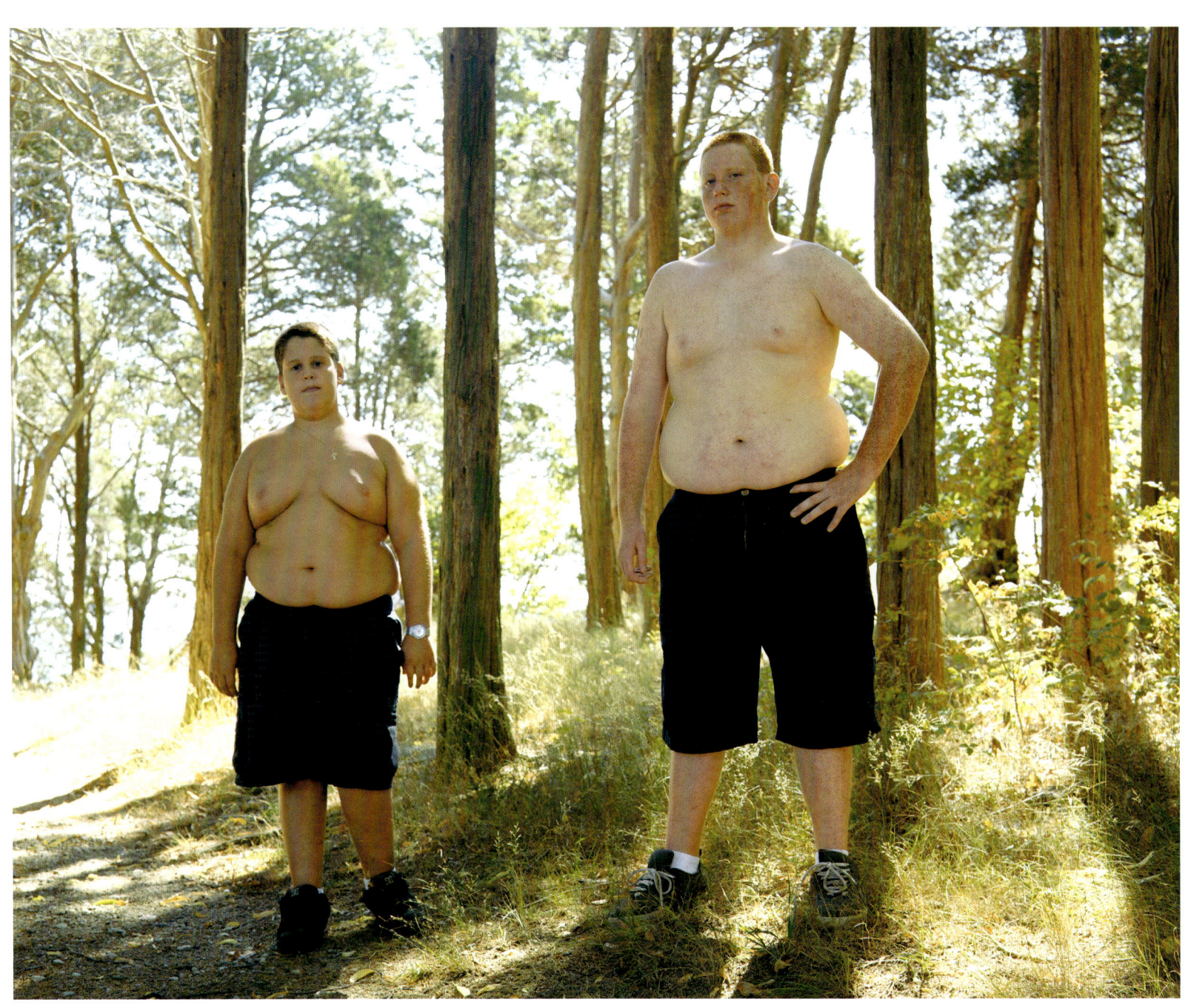

Christopher and Zachary, Bay Farm, Duxbury, MA, 2002

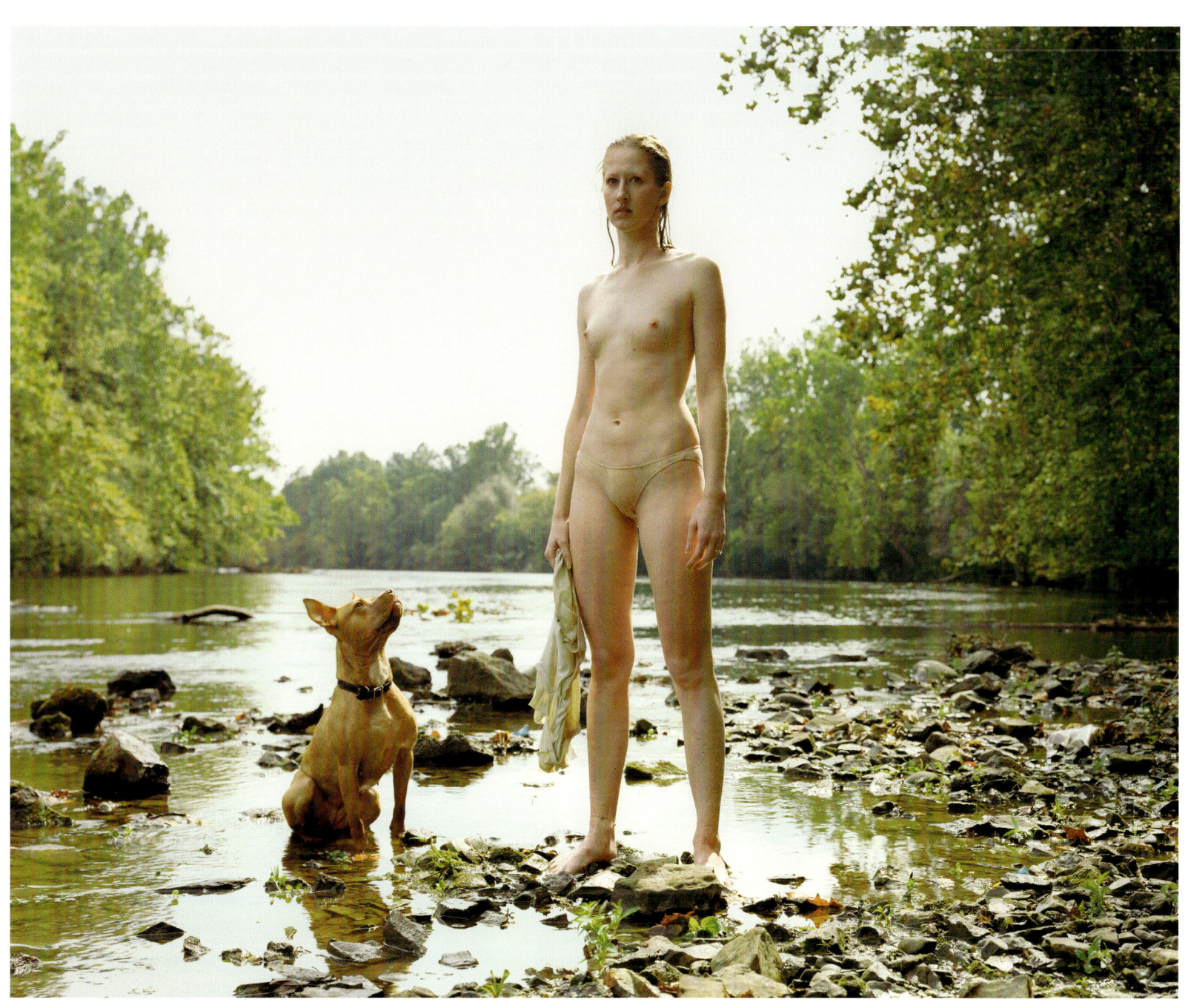

Betty and Angie, Shoeneck Creek, Nazareth, PA, 2003

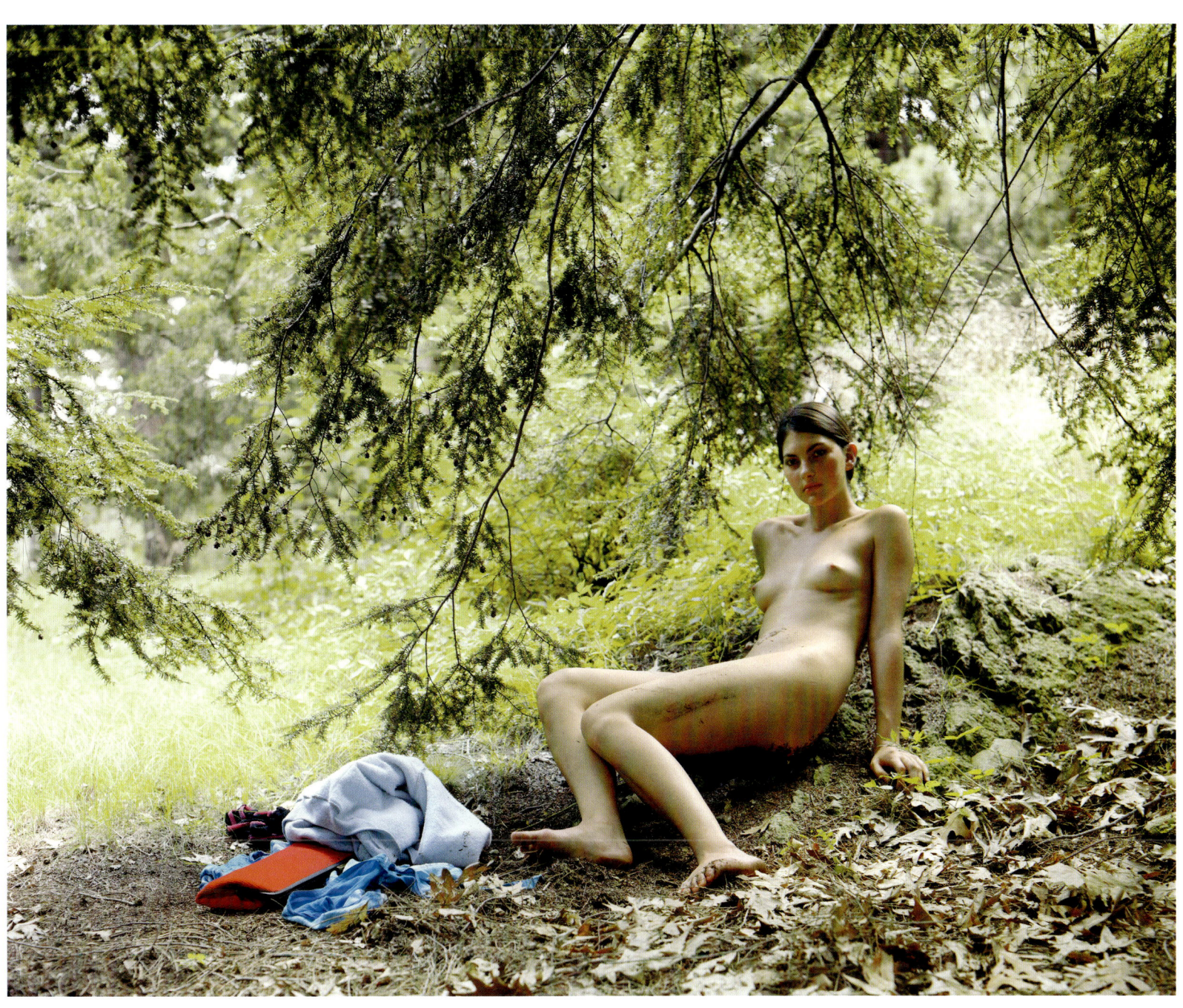

Carla, Arnold Arboretum, Jamaica Plain, MA, 2002

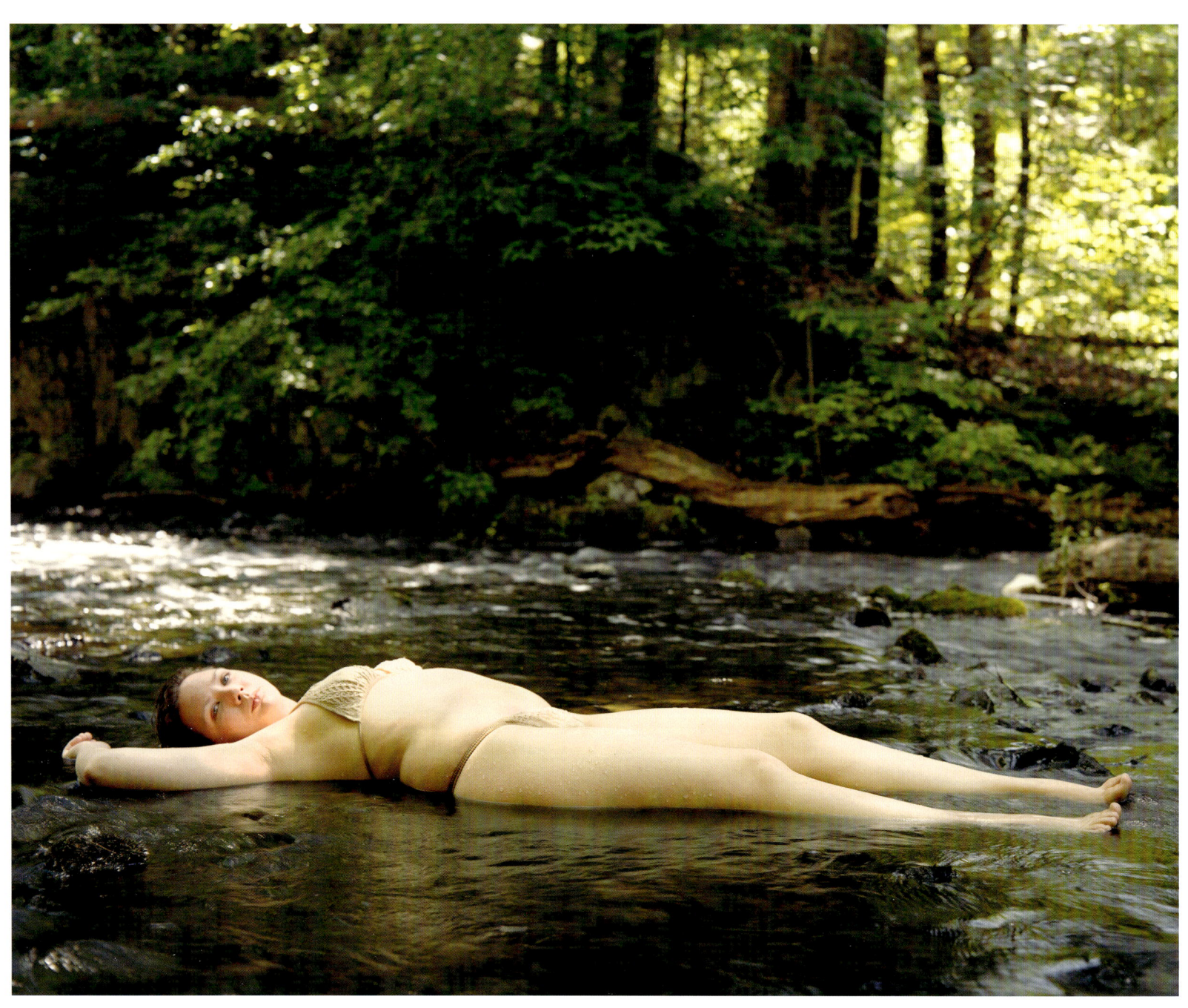

Meghan, Saw Kill River, Annandale, NY, 2002

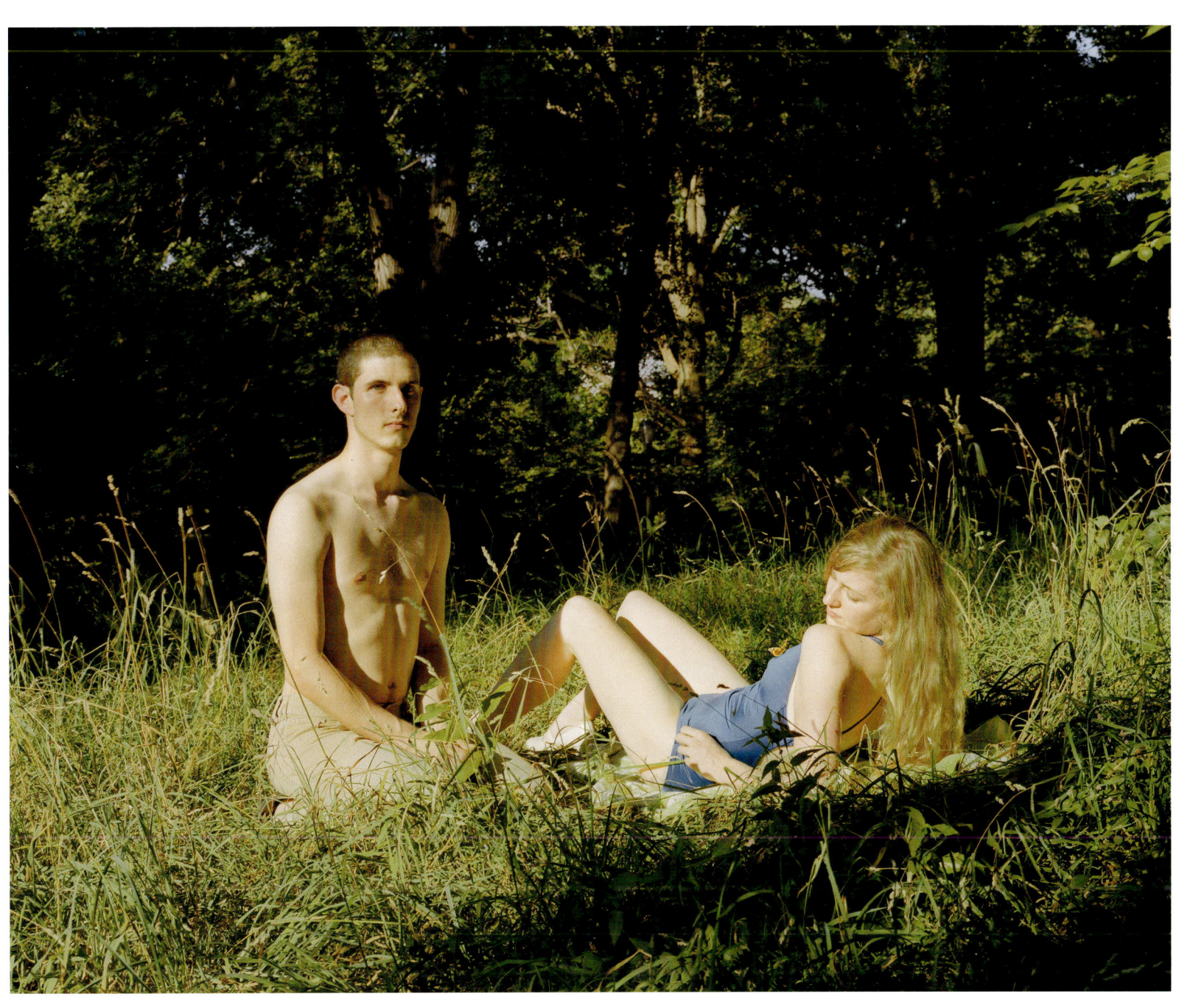

Dee and Van, Prospect Park, Brooklyn, NY, 2003

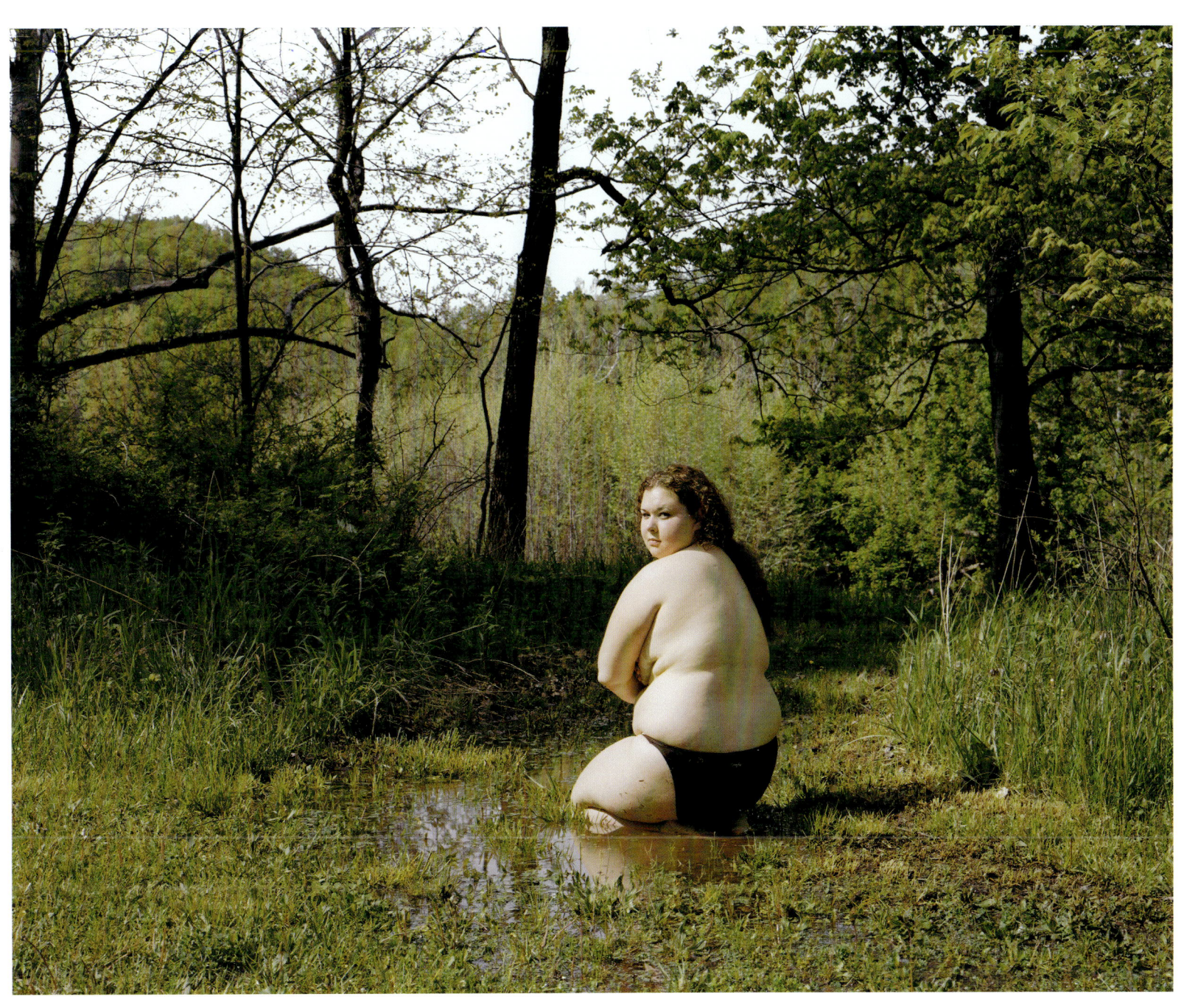

Jada, Sugar Camp Road, Saxton, PA, 2003

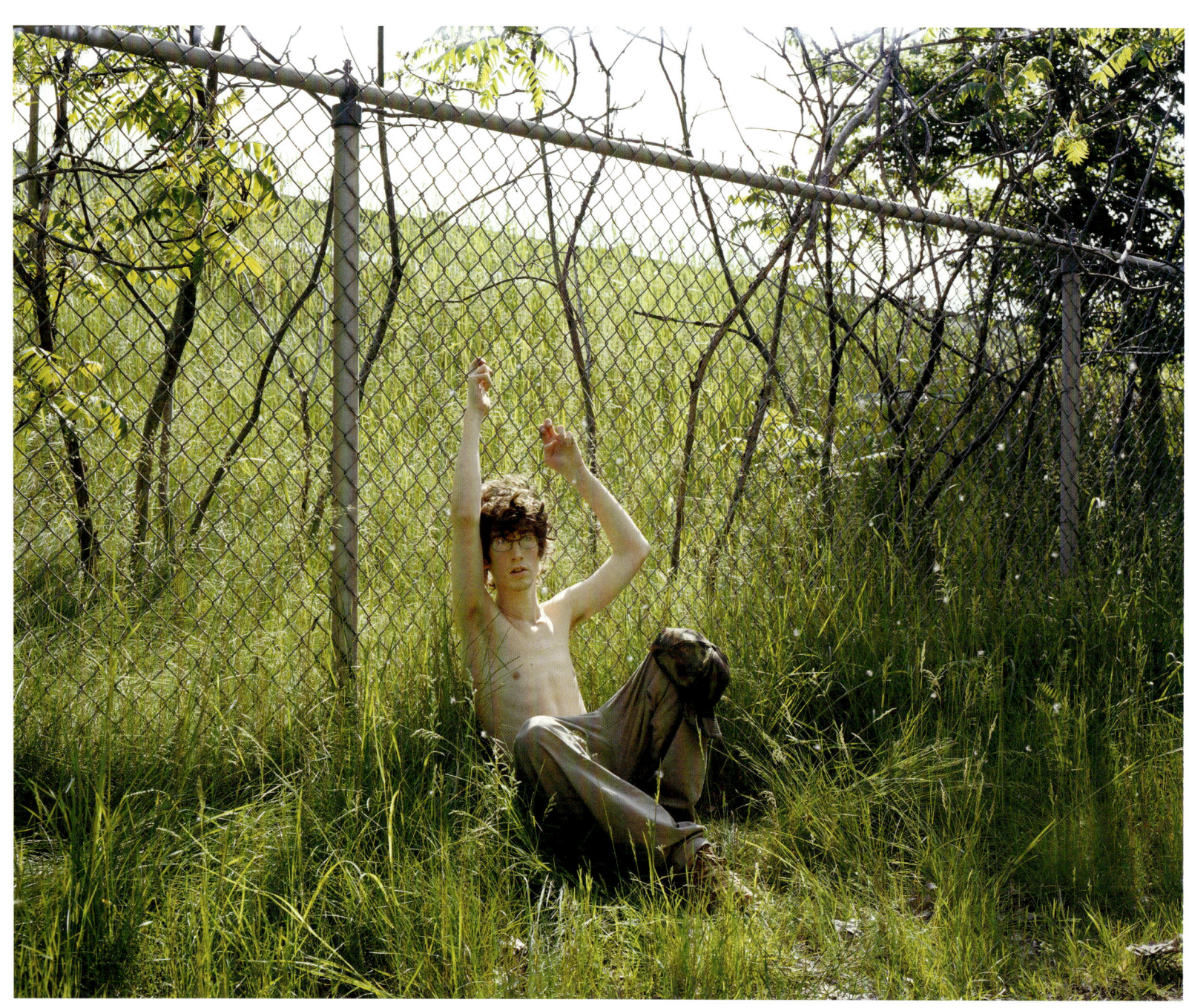

Barton, Route 2, Arlington, MA, 2003

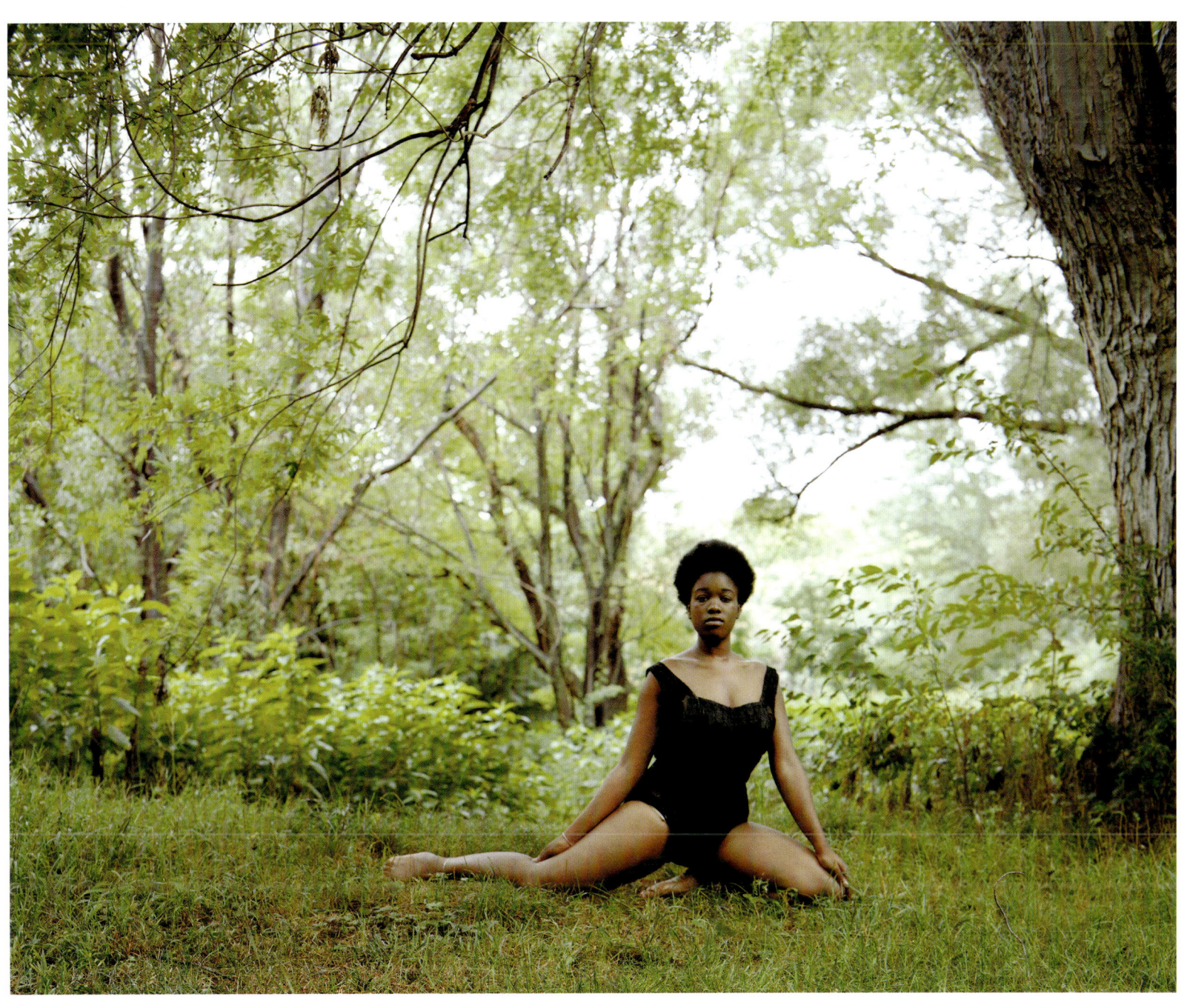

Roberta, Mattapan, MA, 2002

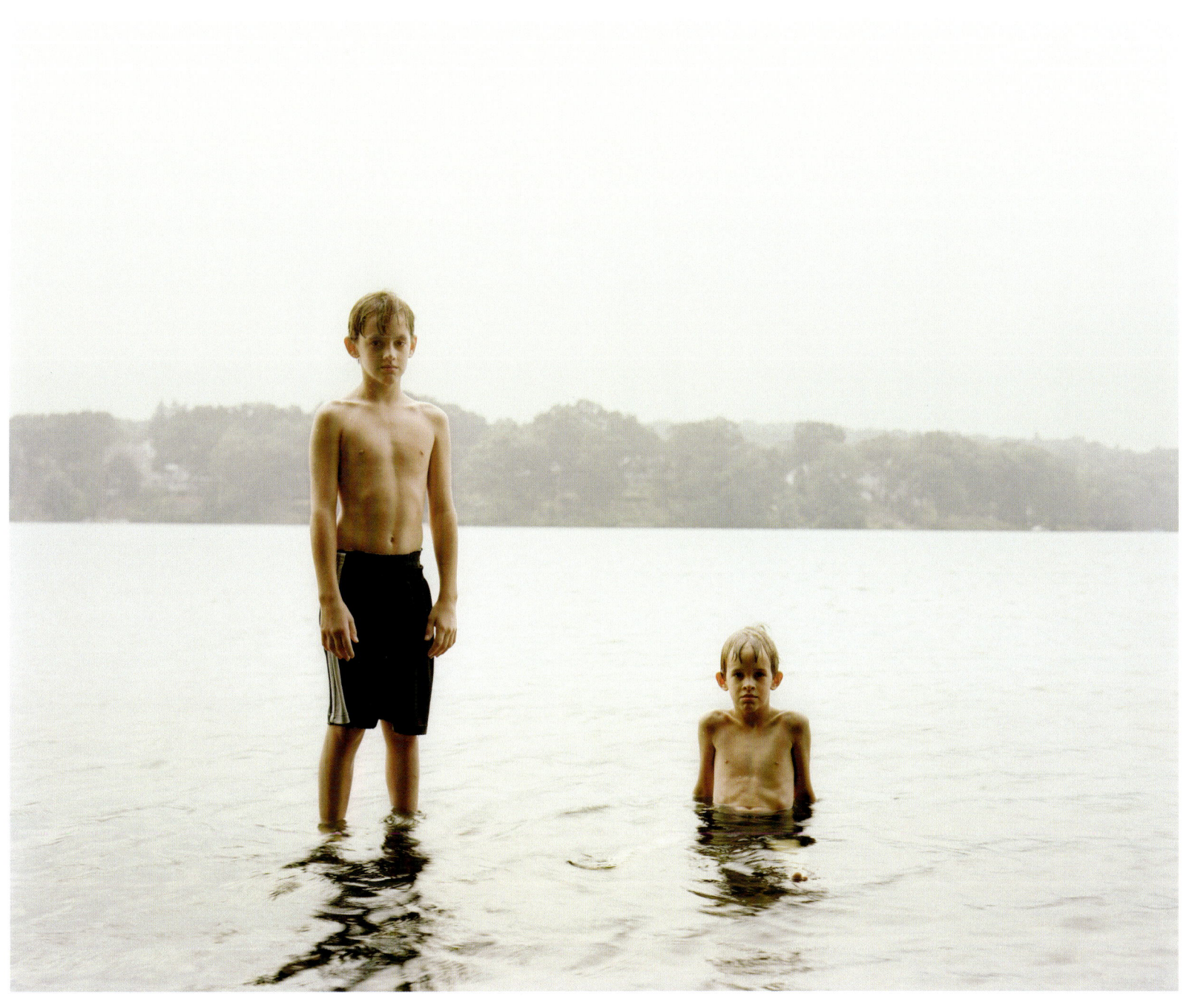

Jessie and Robert, Mystic Lake, Medford, MA, 2002

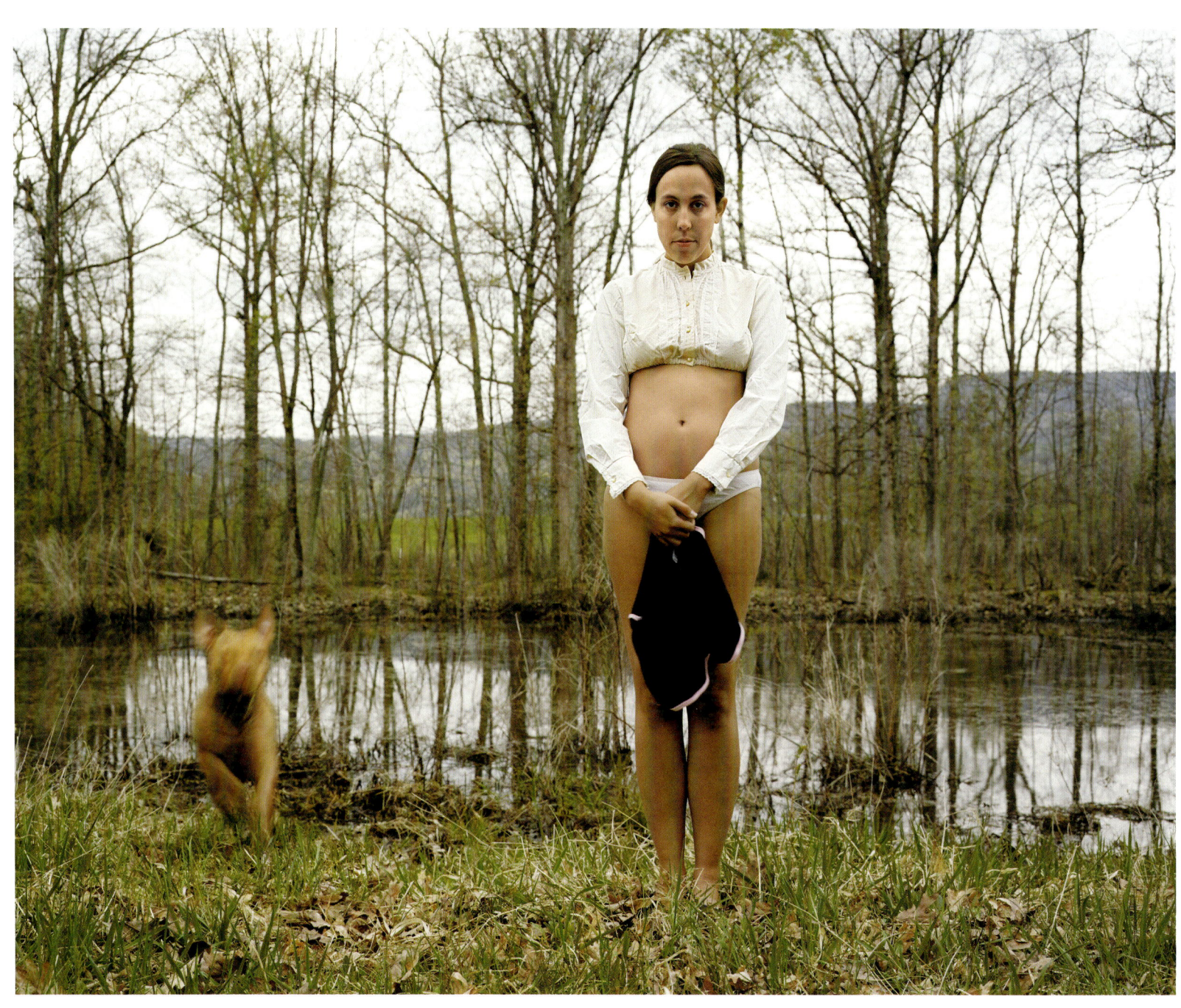

Carla and Pit Bull, Gate House Road, New Paltz, NY, 2003

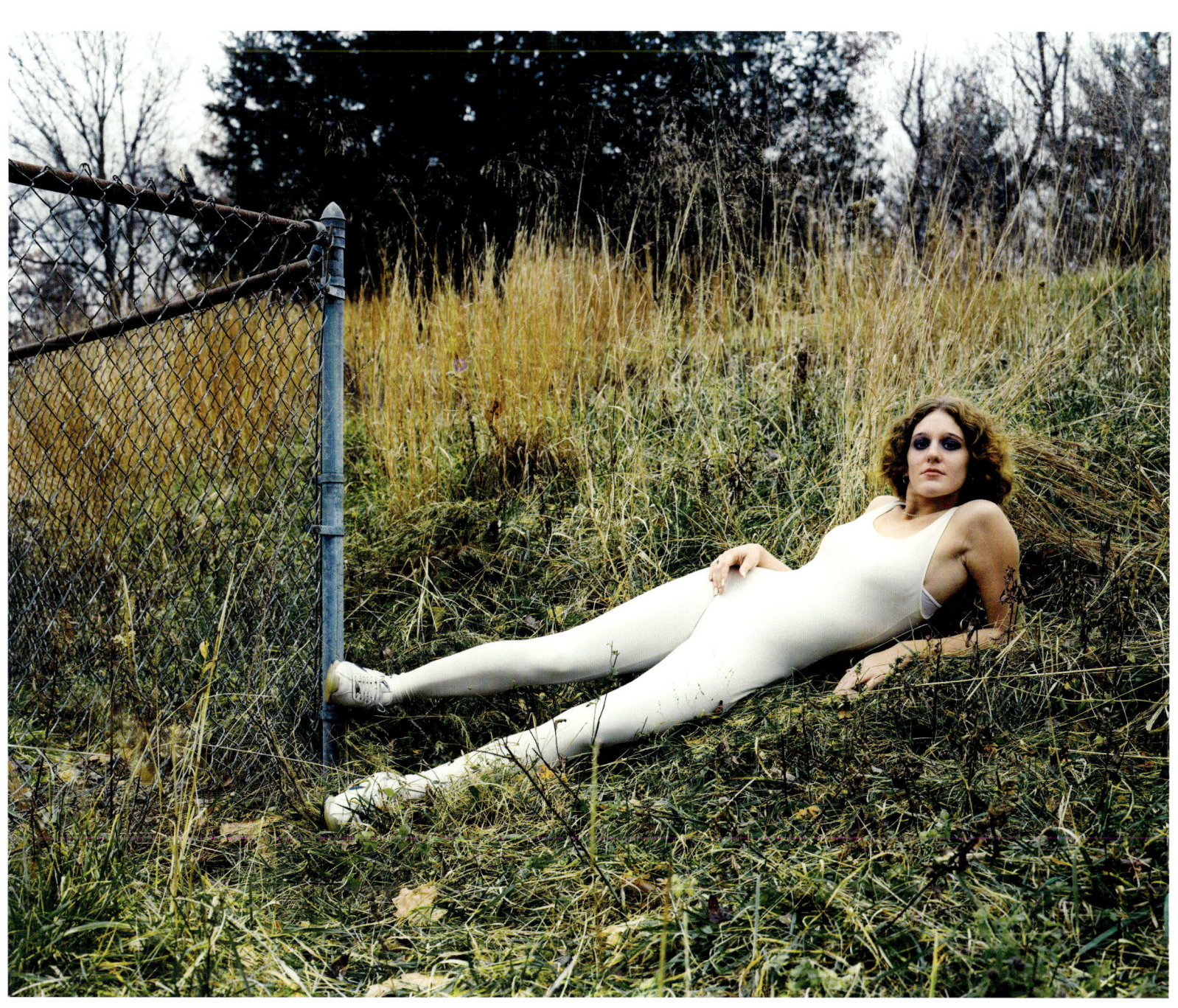

Danielle, Vacant Lot, Burleigh Road, New Paltz, NY, 2003

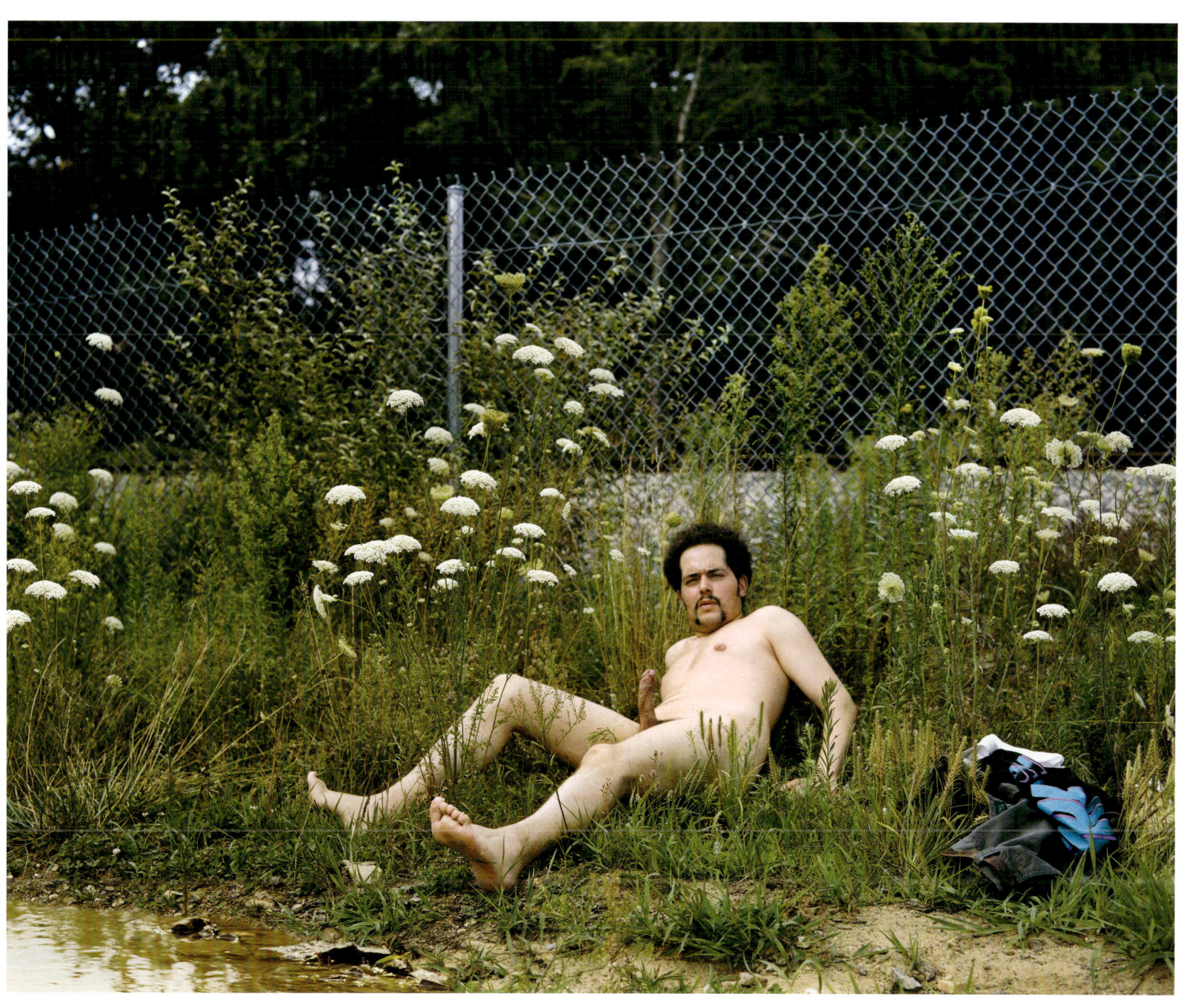

Robert, Christmas Tree Farm, Kingston, MA, 2002

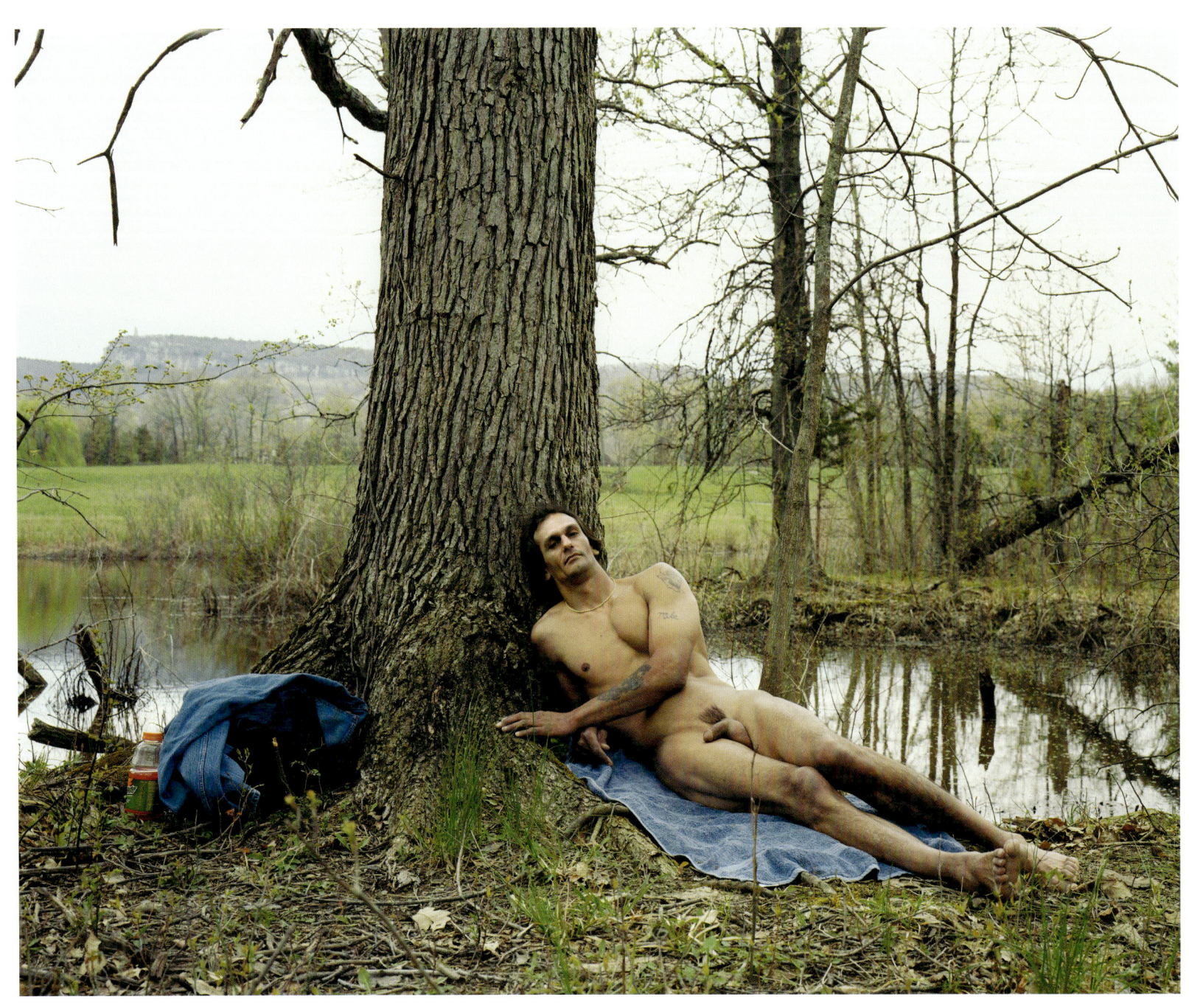

Mike, Private Property, New Paltz, NY, 2003

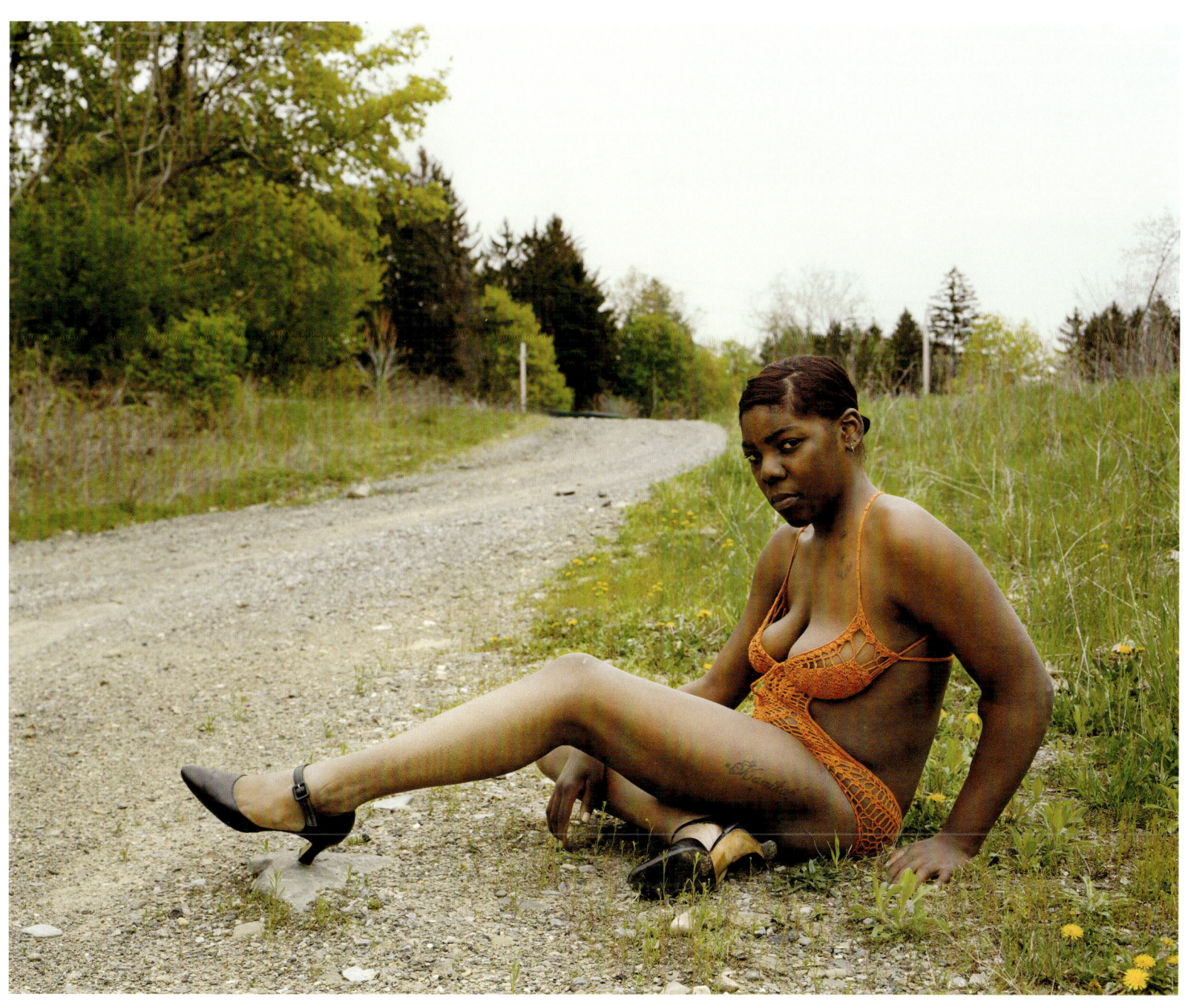

Kamika, Near Route 9, Poughkeepsie, NY, 2003

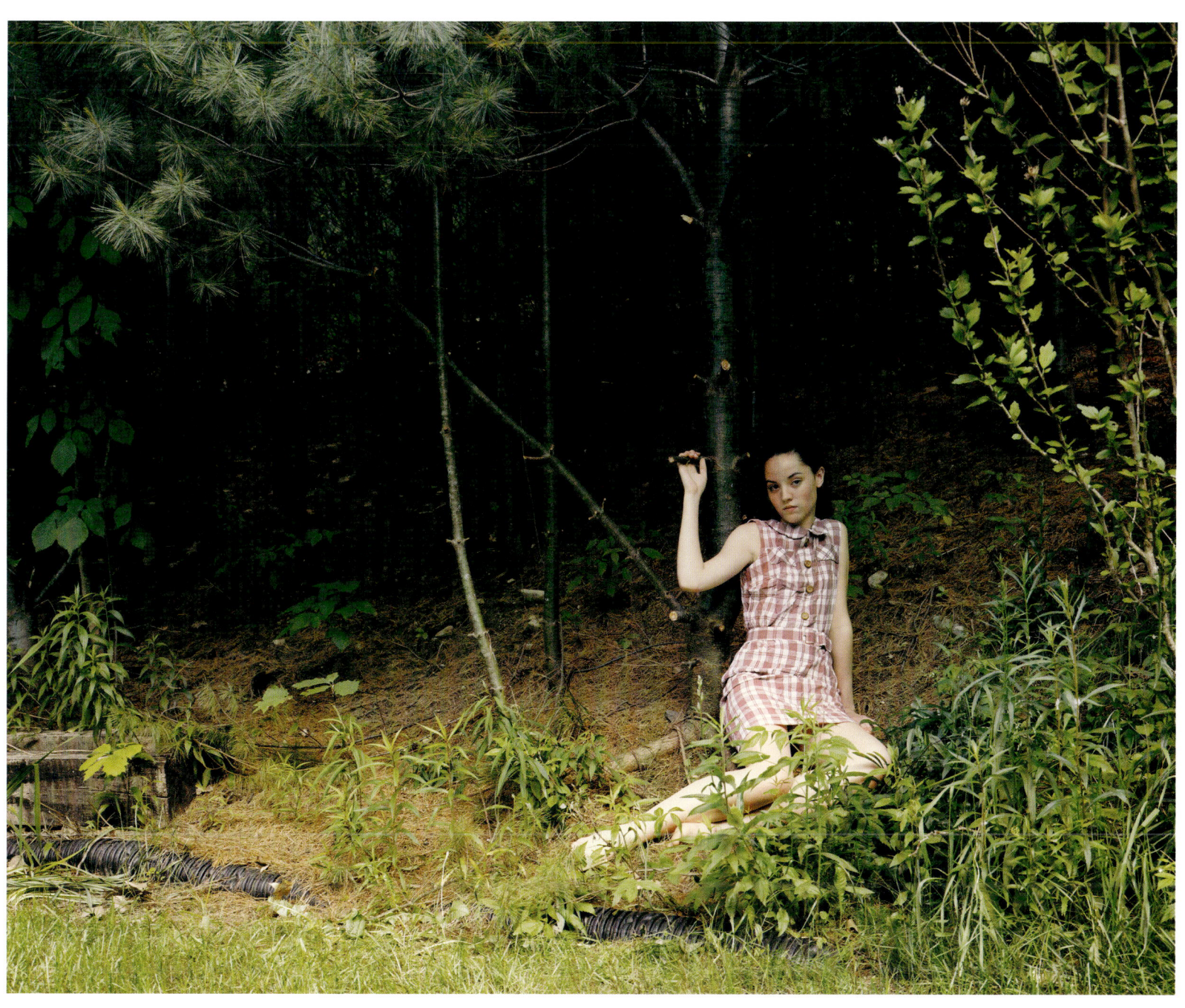

Taryn, Riddle Brook, Pinardville, NH, 2003

"Me and Bobby McGee" blared in the distance as C. and I walked through the woods toward the water. I'd been to this location over and over again, but this was the first time I found someone else there. It was 9 a.m. and strange to hear so much noise so early near the pretty houses on the lake. I expected to find some kids fishing or swimming but instead saw a group of adults gathered near the shore. We stepped over one man who was passed out on the pathway. Another, a woman, sat on a rock staring in our direction, oblivious. All morning the music played loud as they danced and fought, tossing empty beer bottles and wet clothes onto the grass, not far from where I stood photographing C.   **MYSTIC LAKE**, 2004

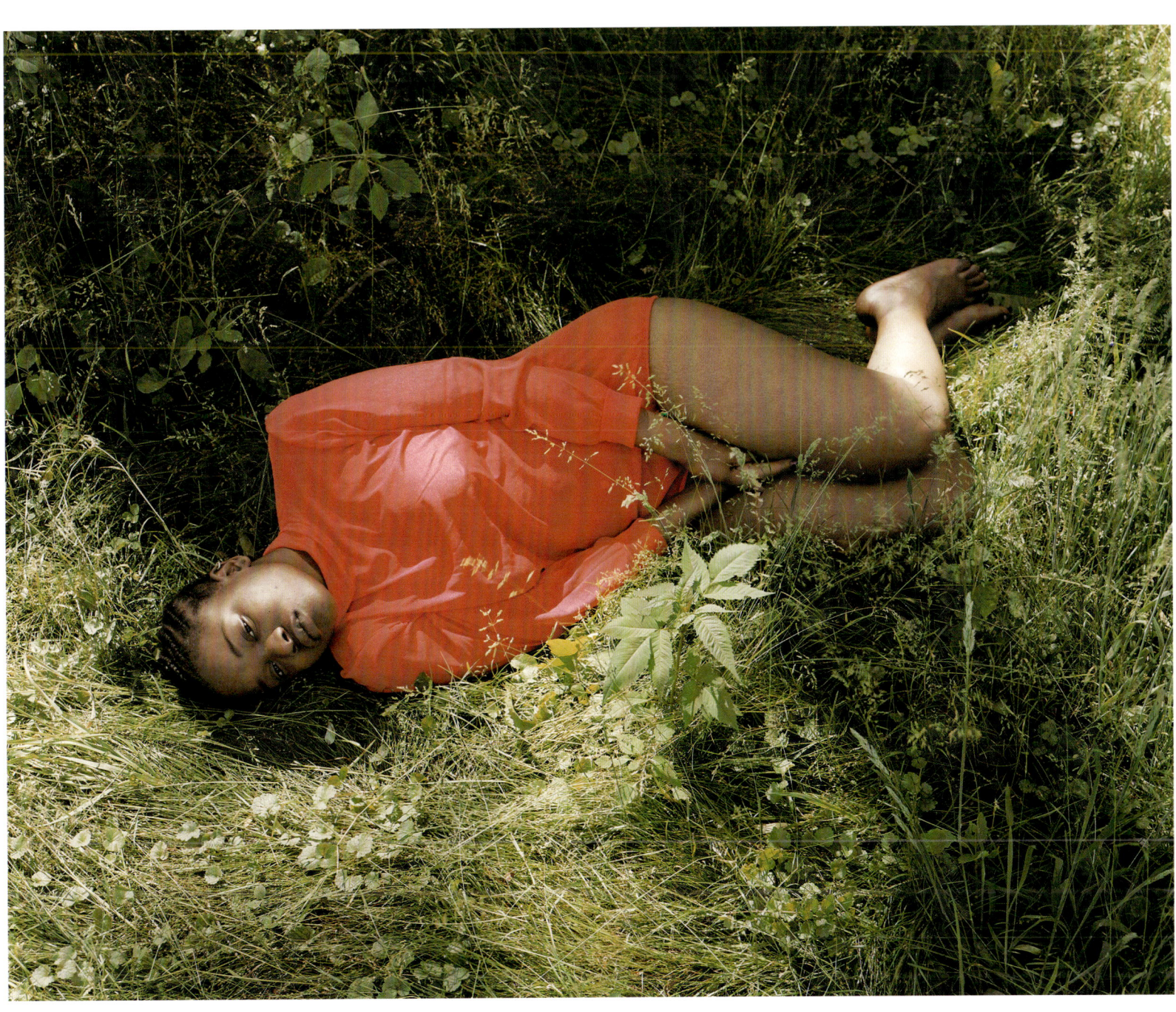

Roberta, b. 1981

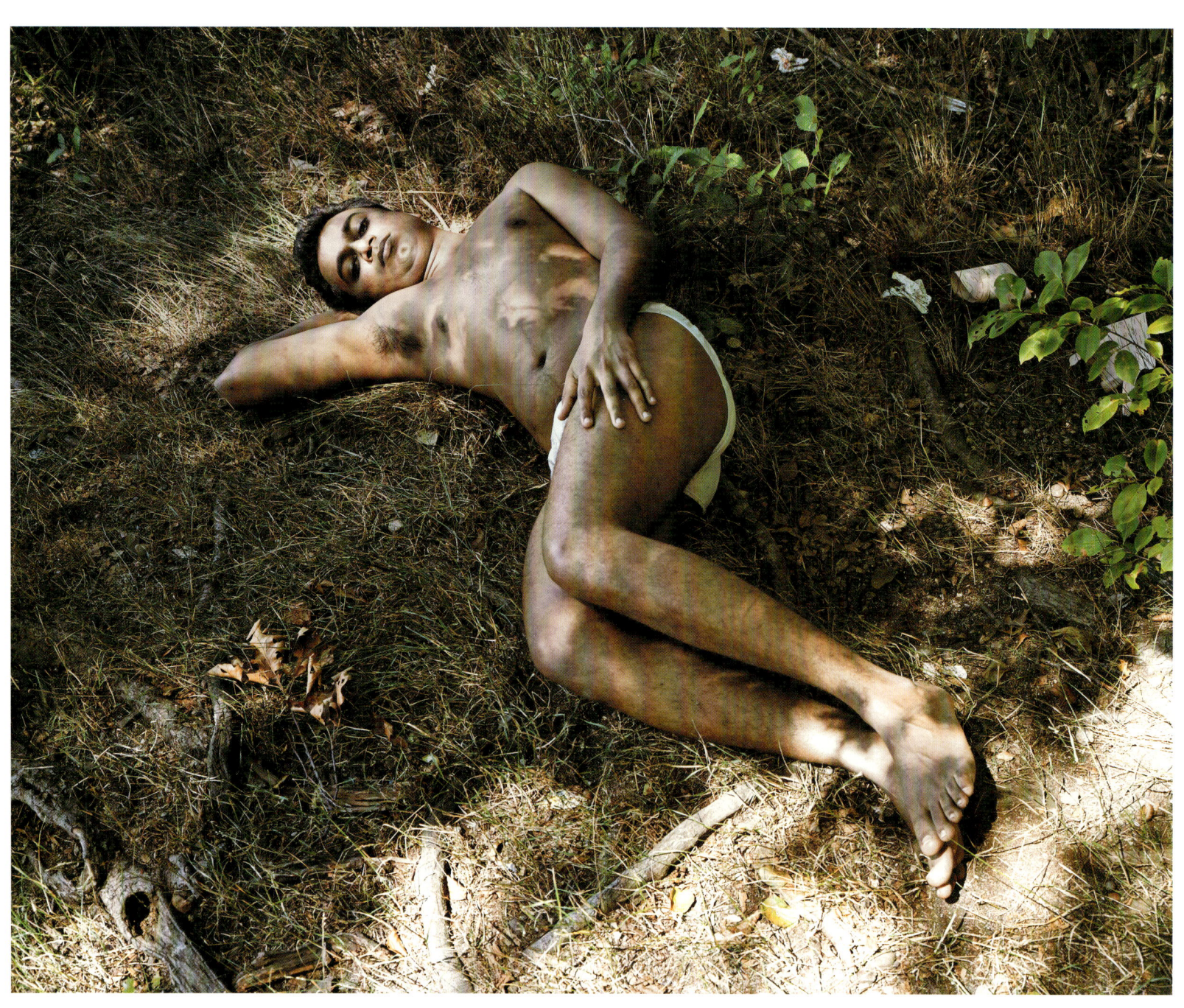

Reuben, b. 1976

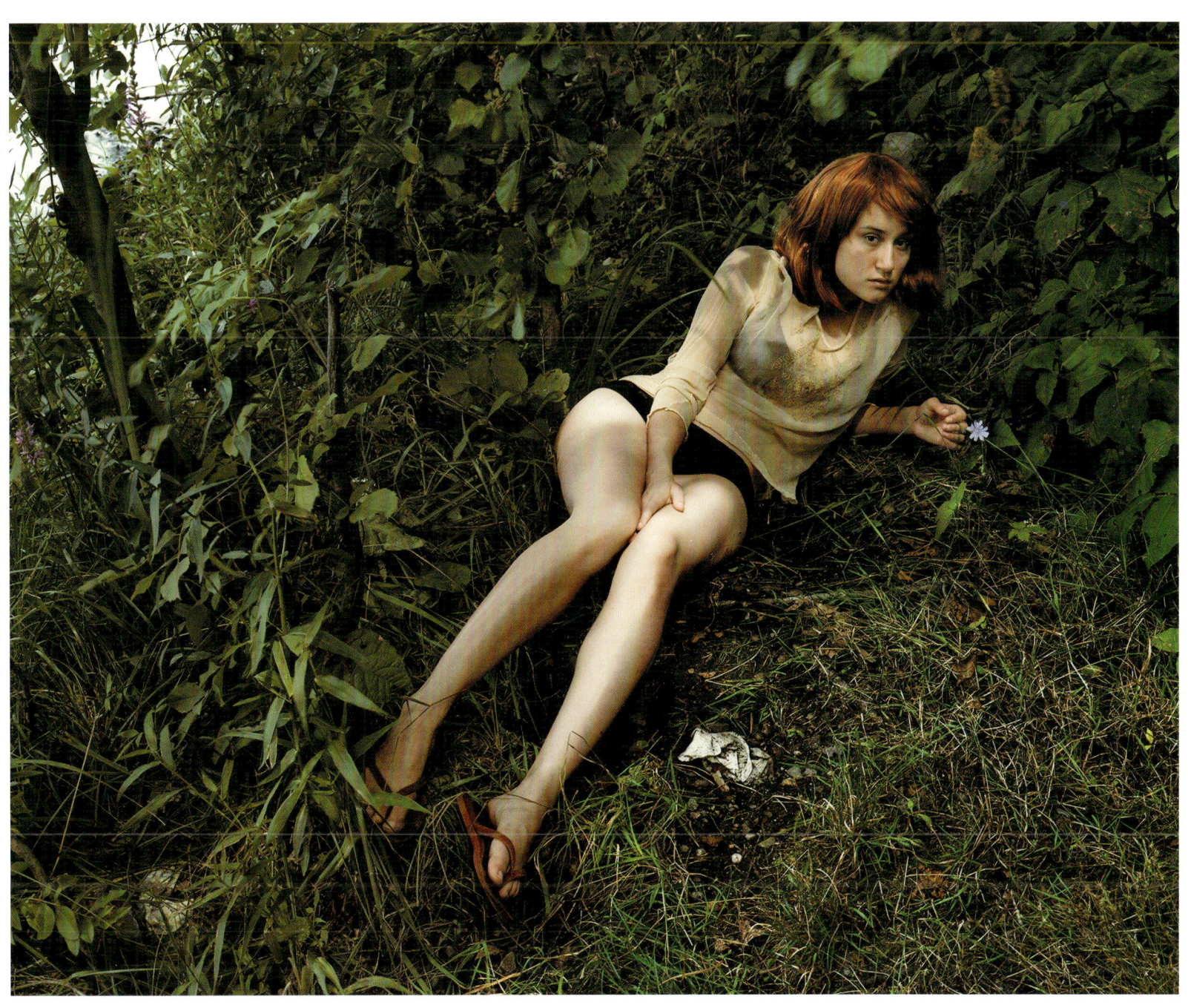

Cassandra, b. 1983

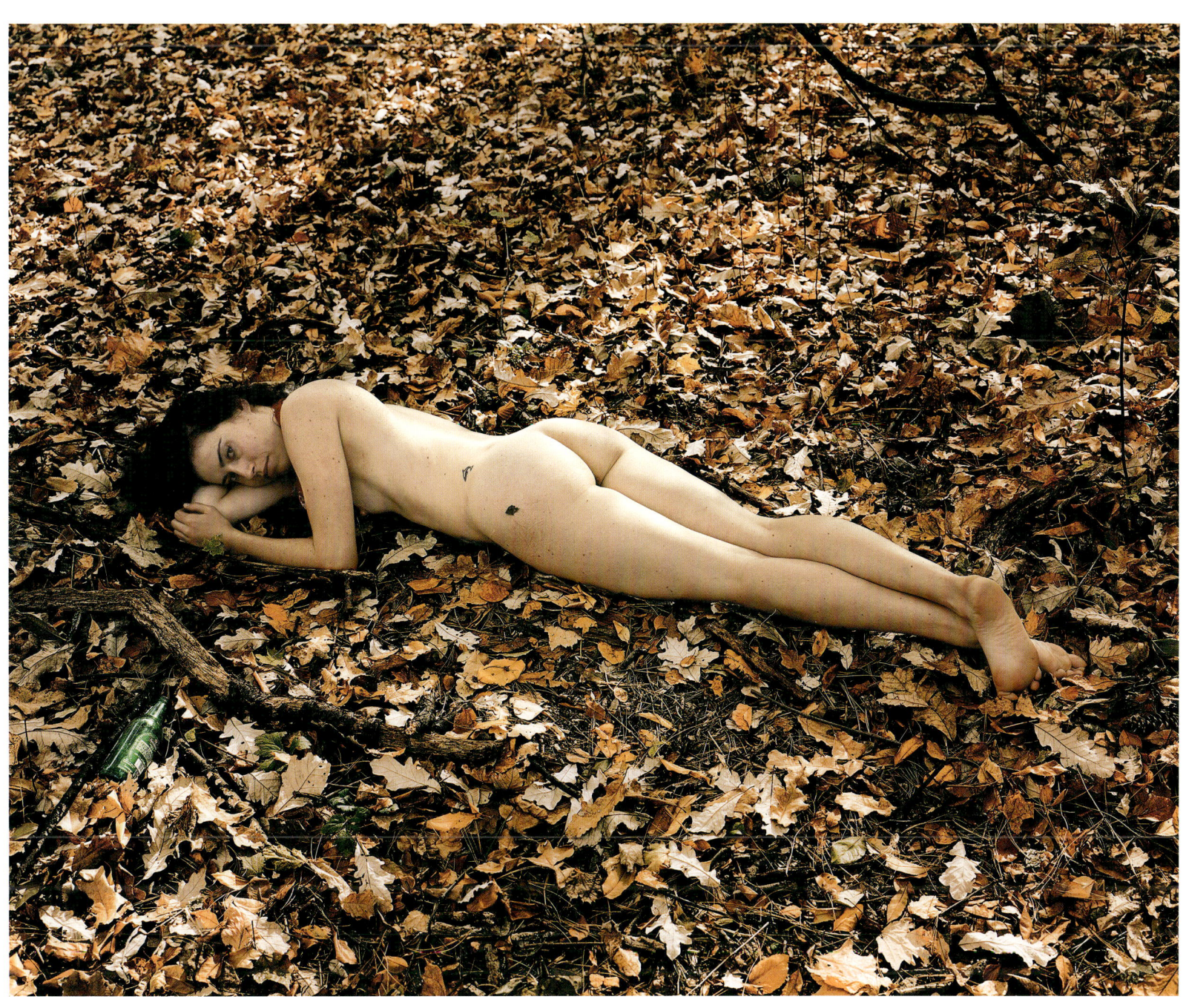

Michele, b. 1977

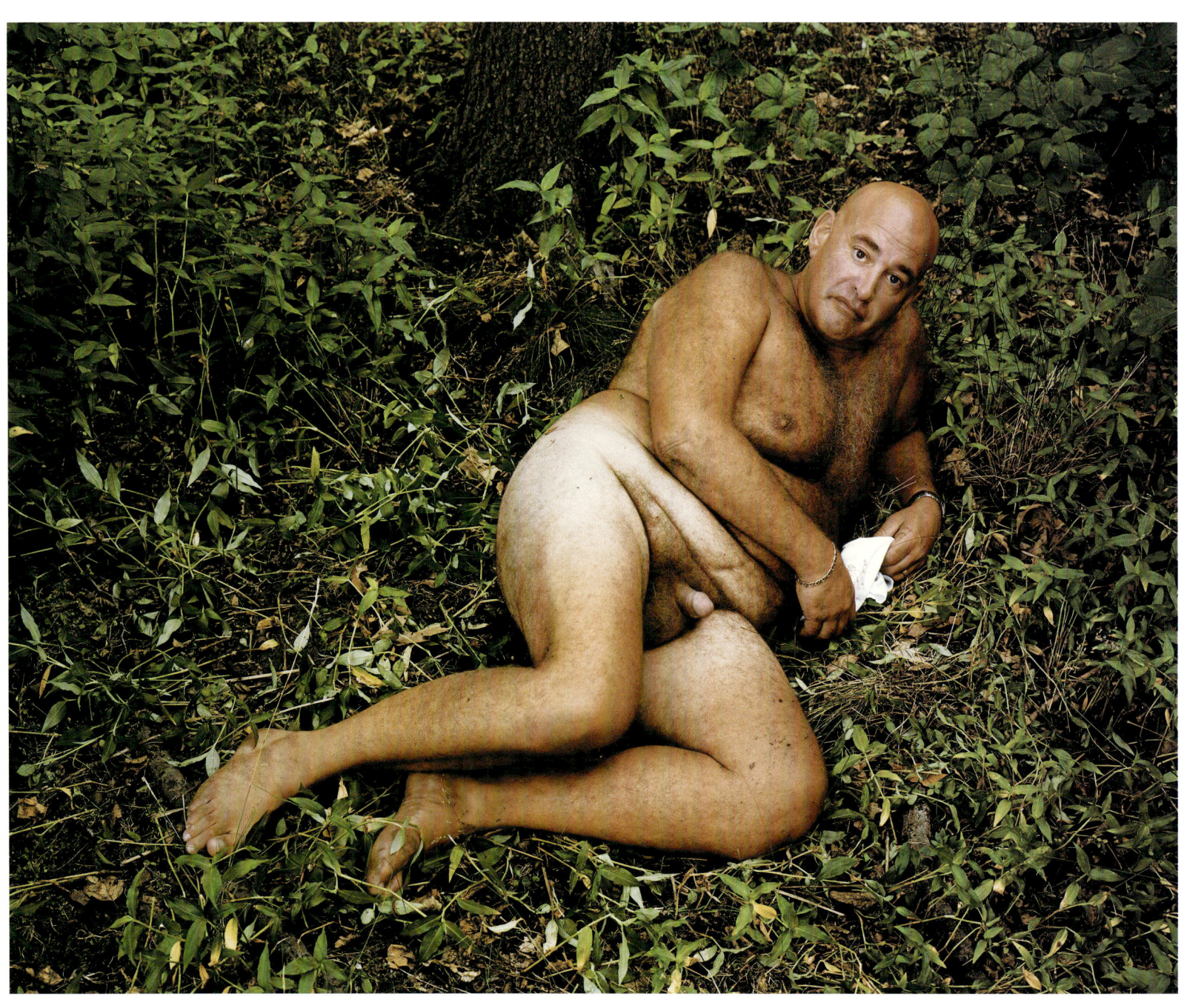

Allen, b. 1951

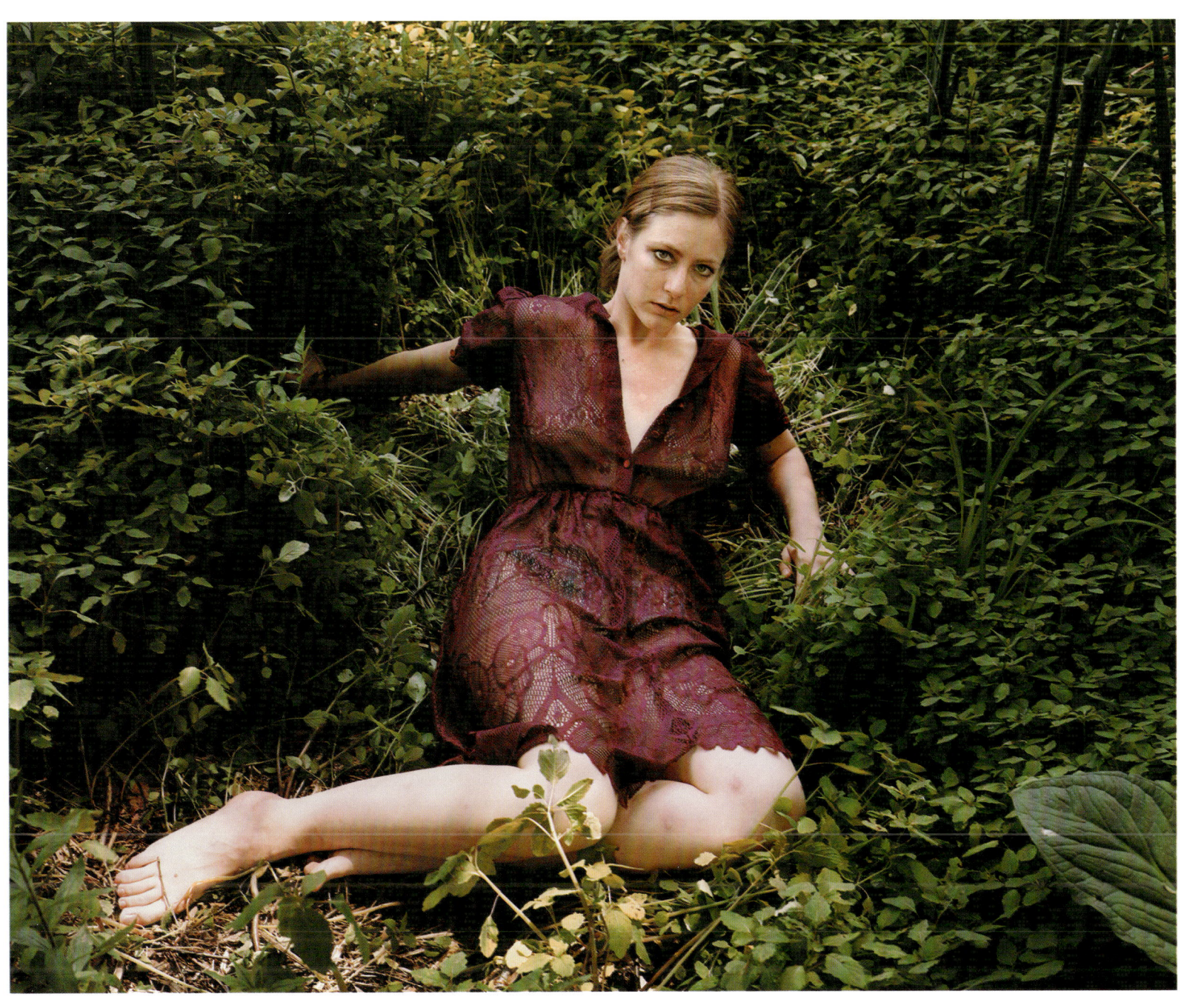

Carolyn, b. 1982

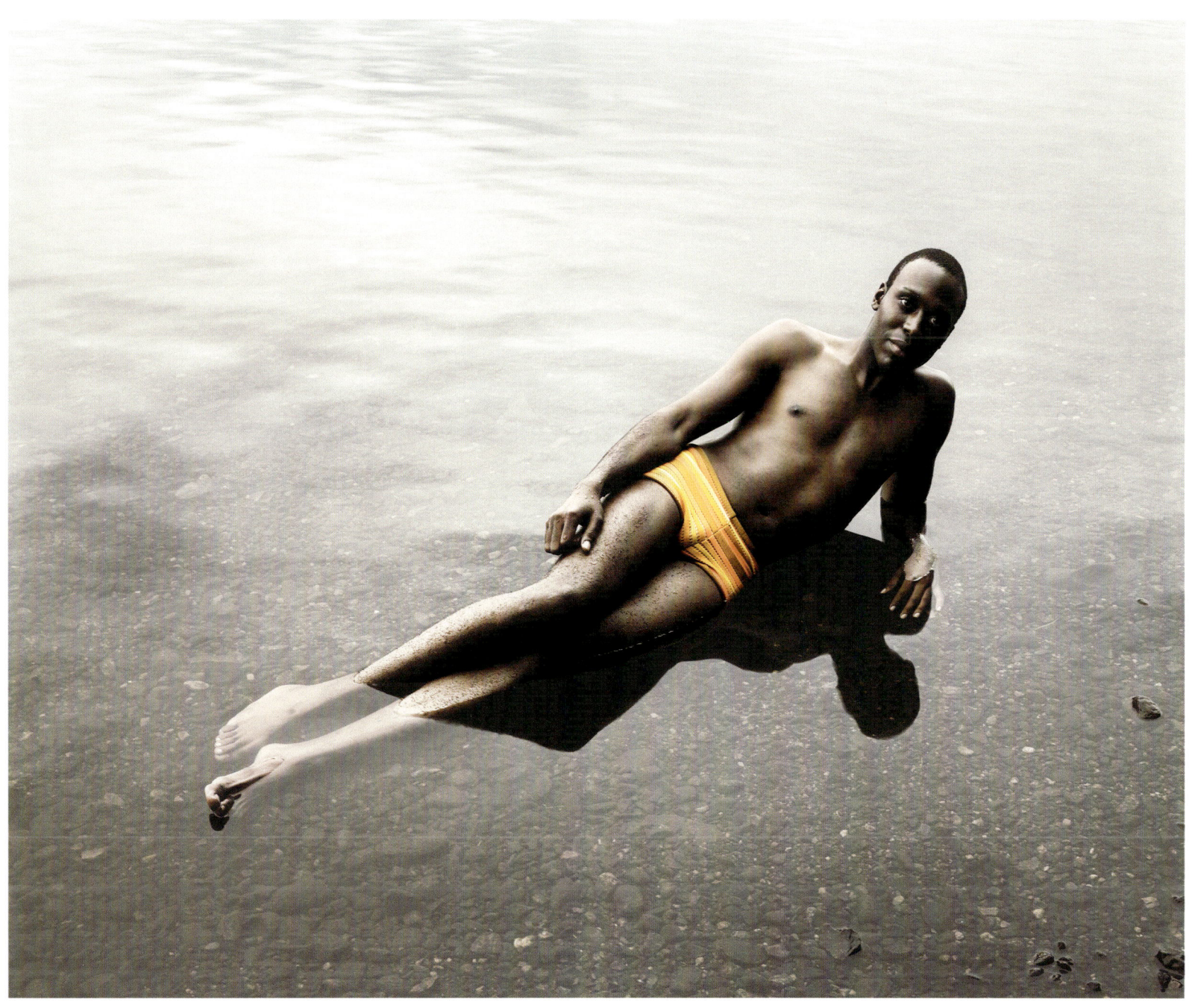

Tim, b. 1981

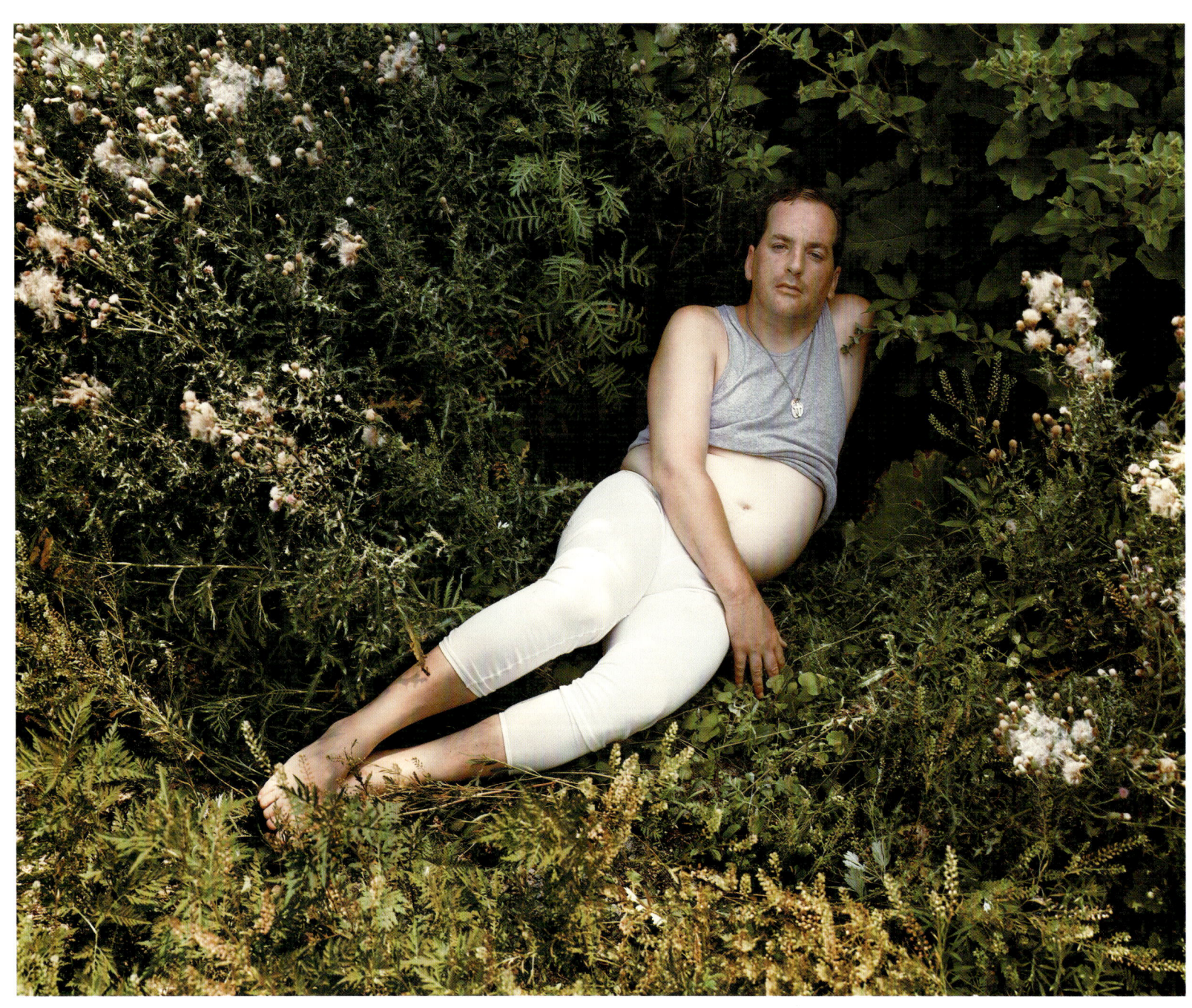

Paul, b. 1969

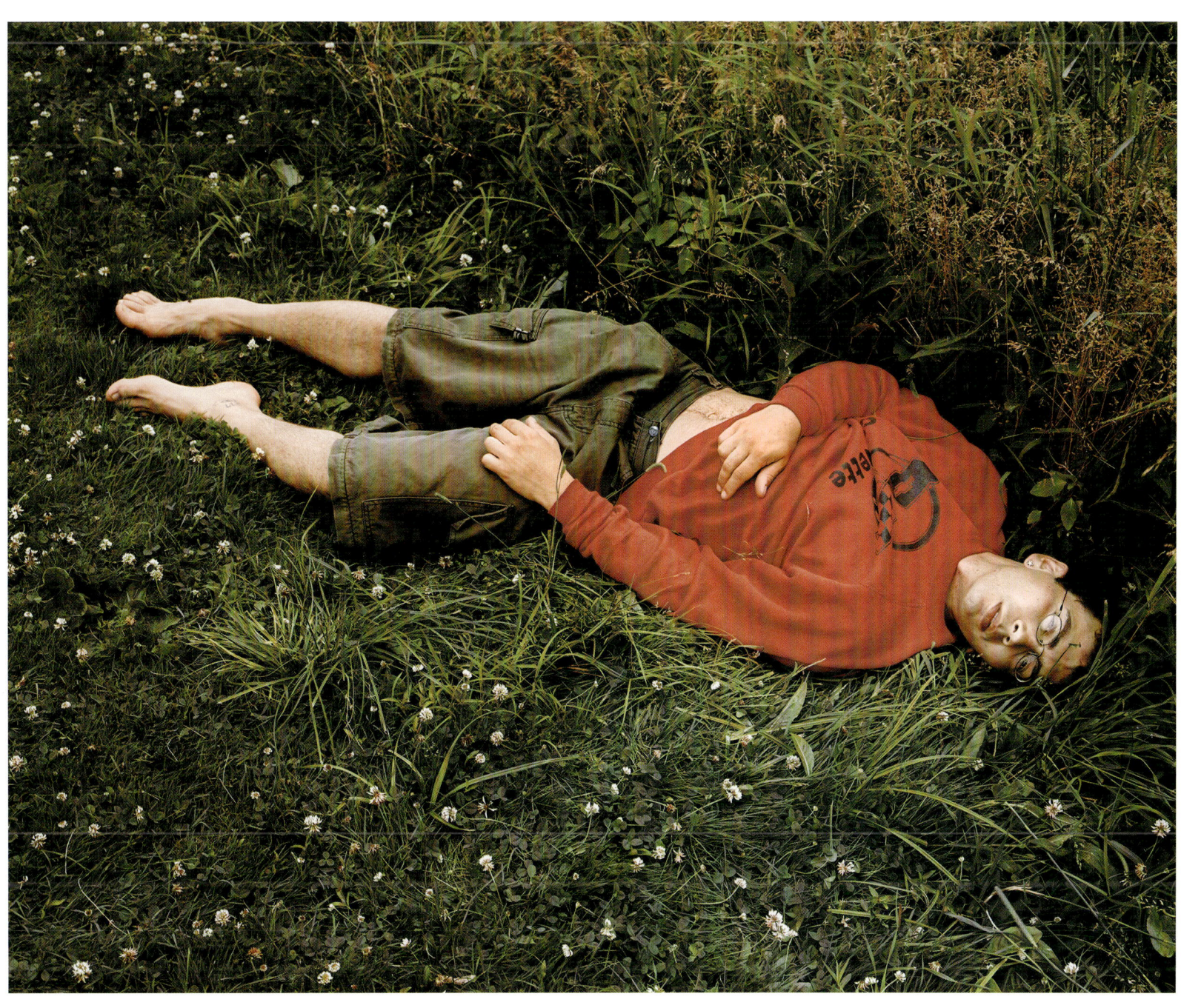

Andrew, b. 1975

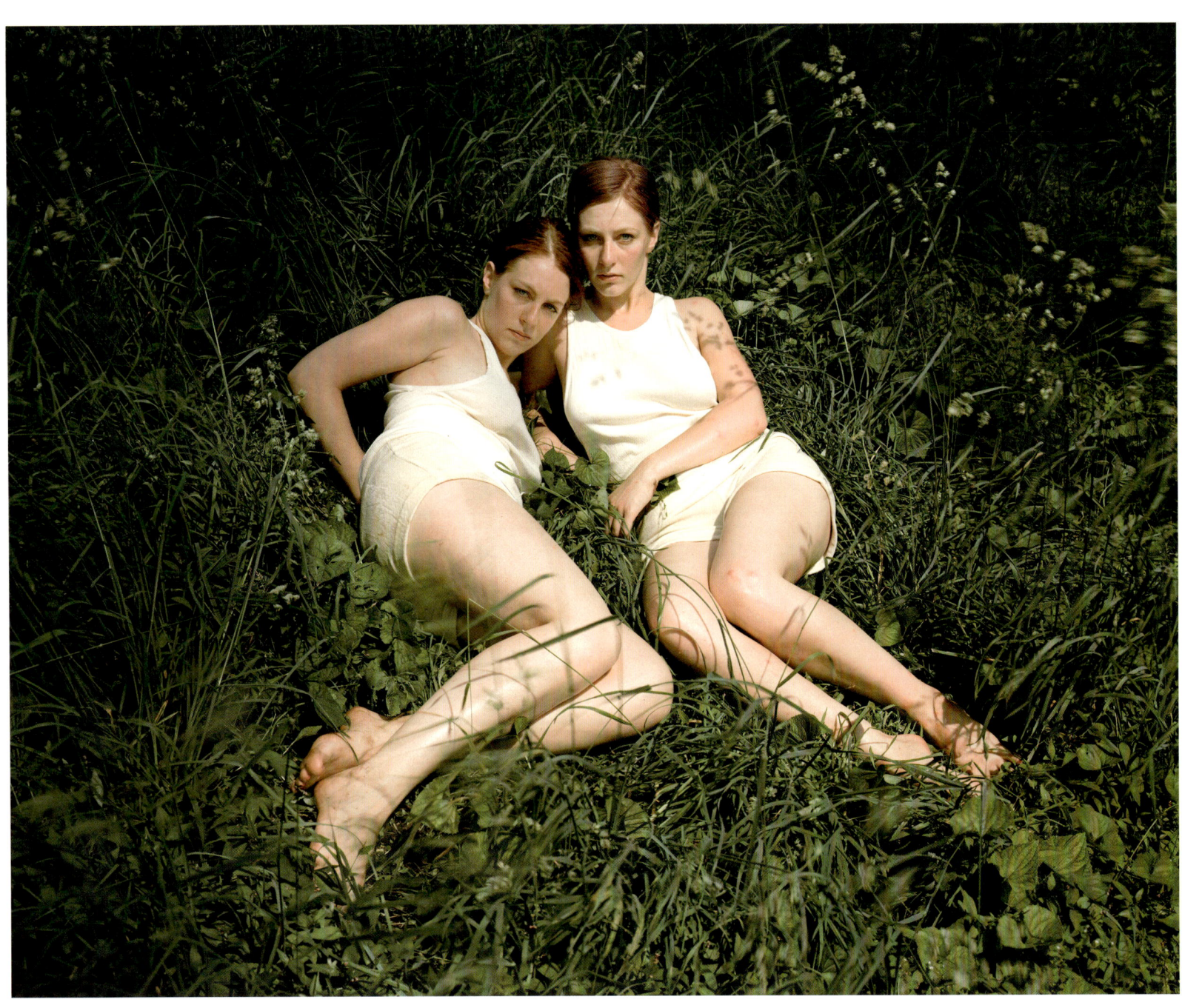

Carolyn and Catherine, b. 1982

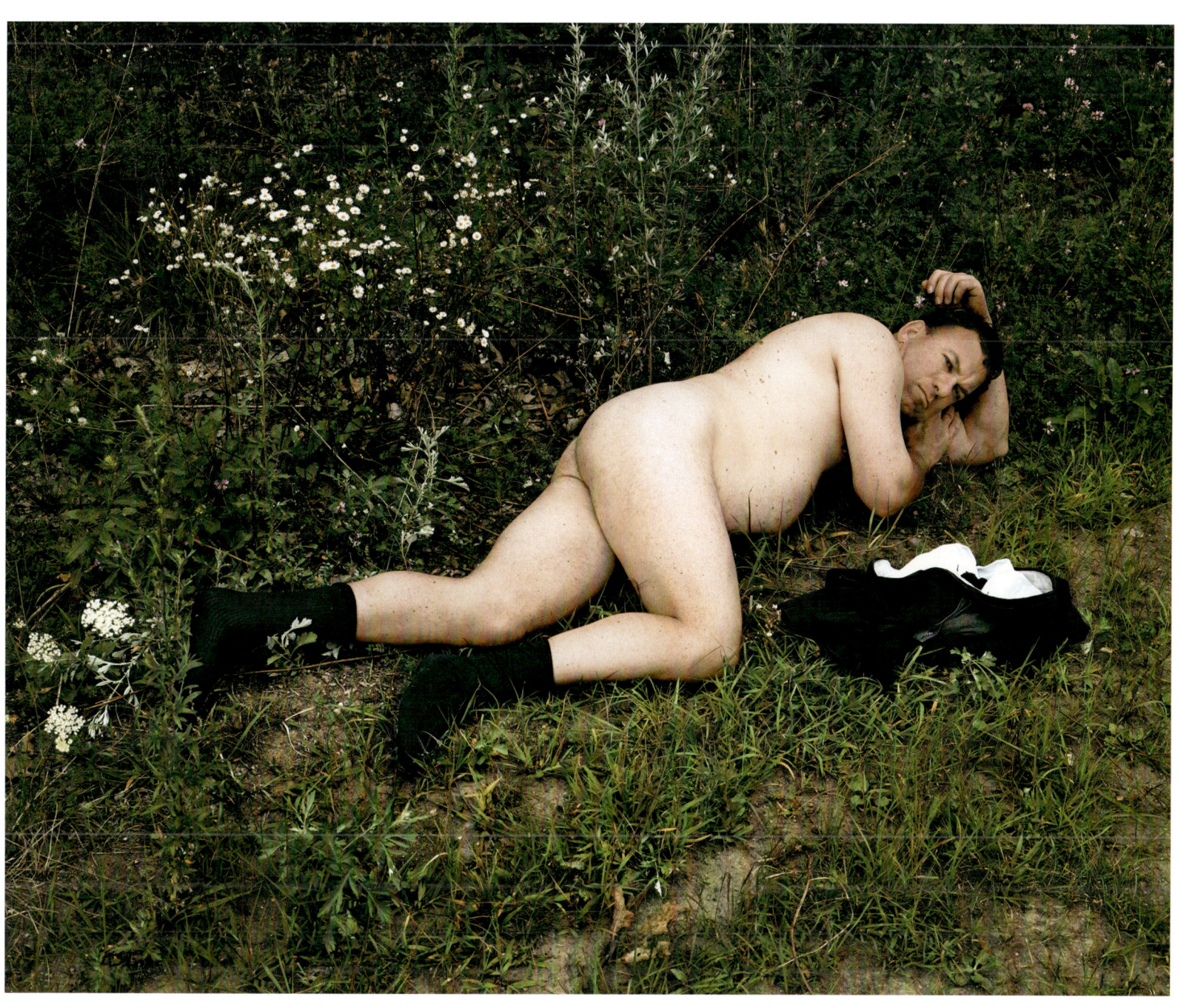

Ken, b. 1961

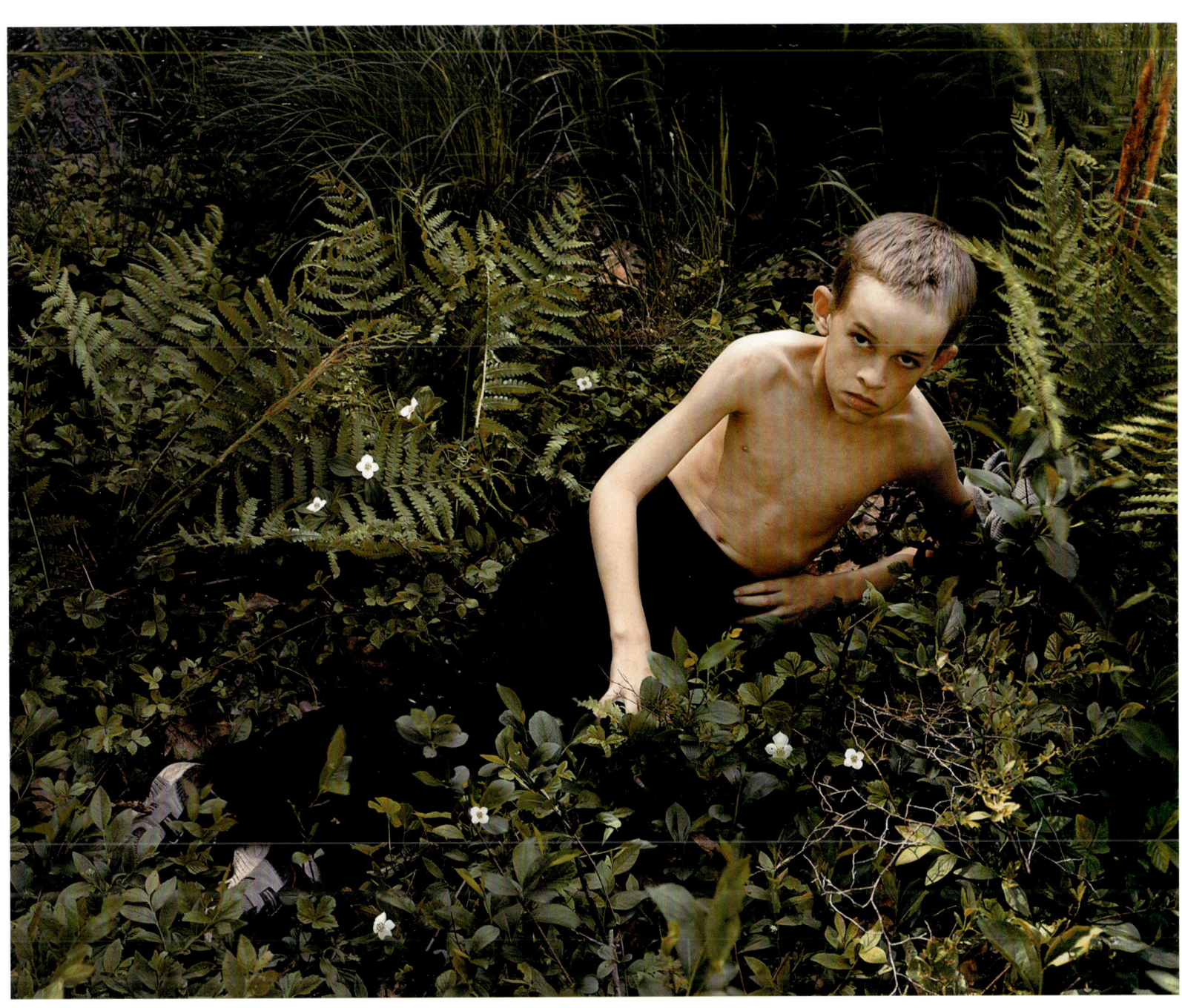

Robbie, b. 1994

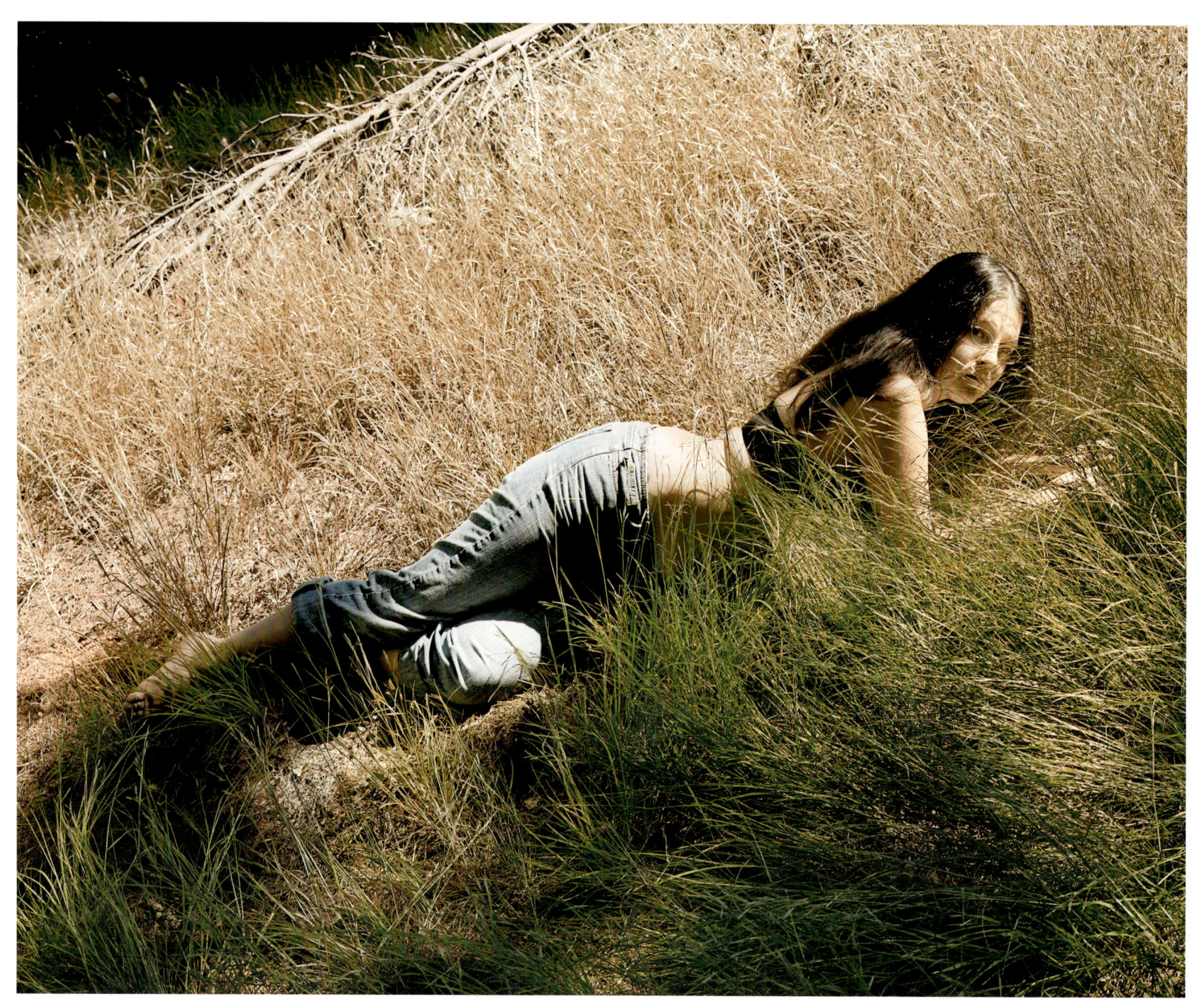

Addie, b. 1980

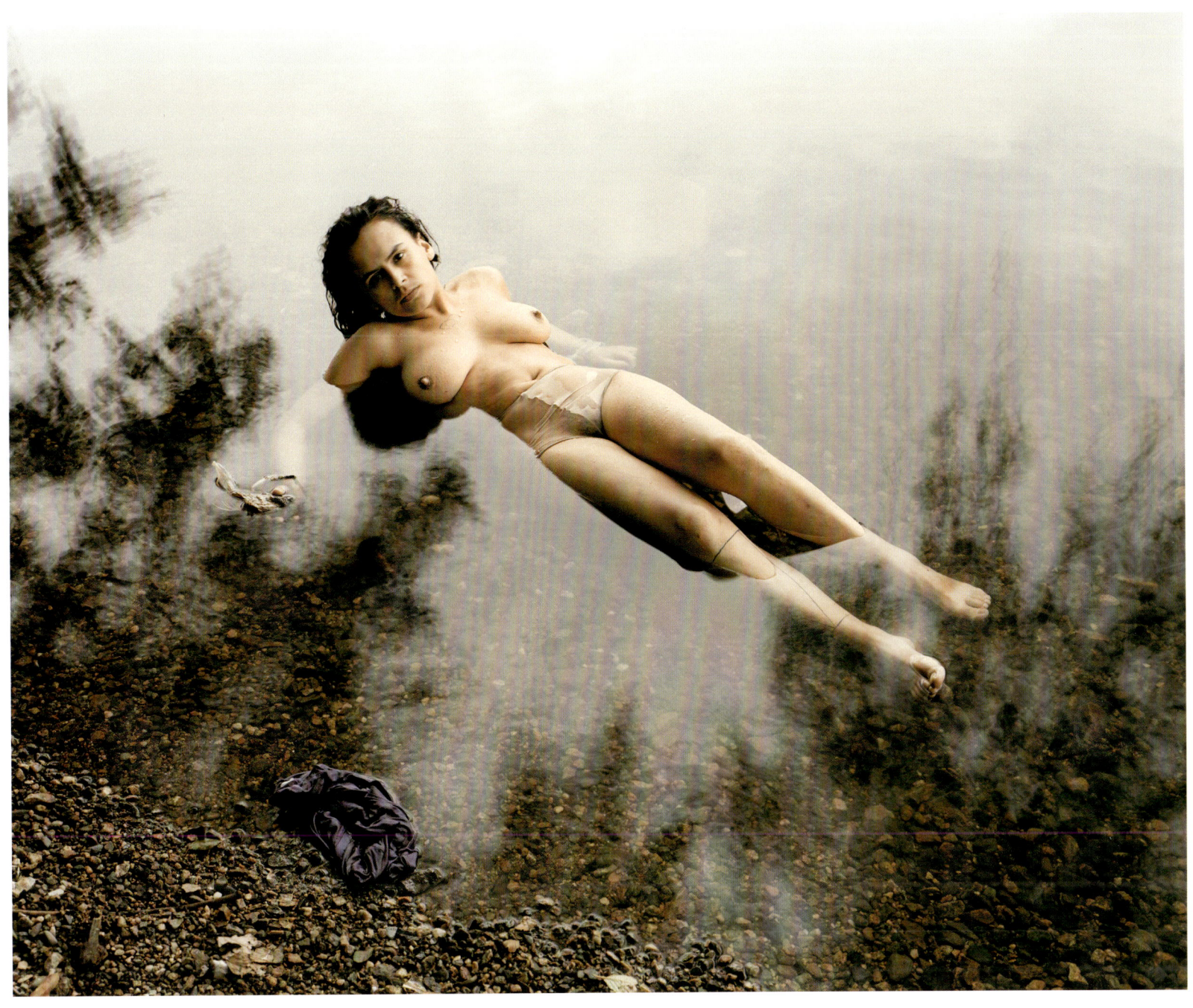

Jaime, b. 1970

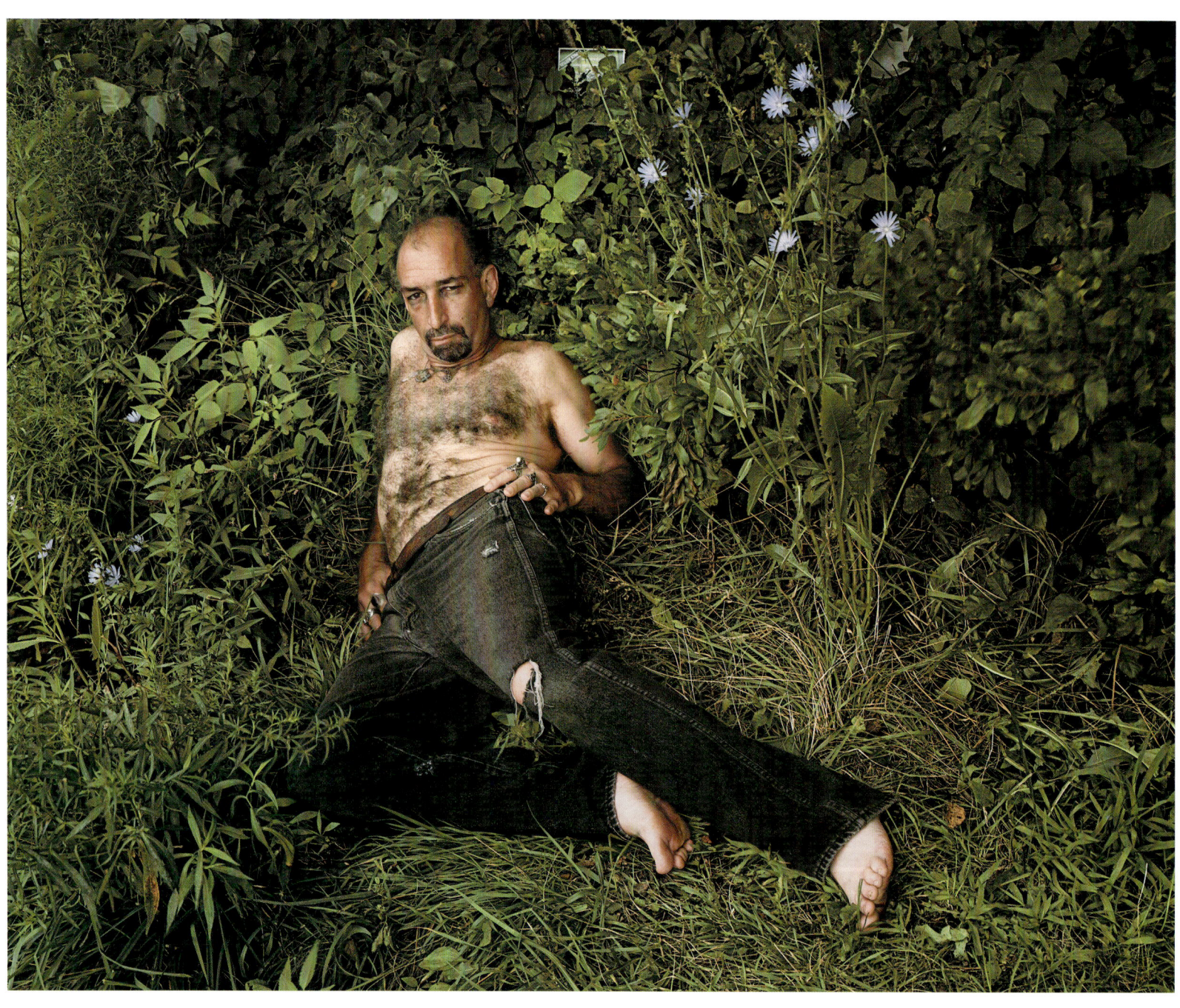

Frank, b. 1956

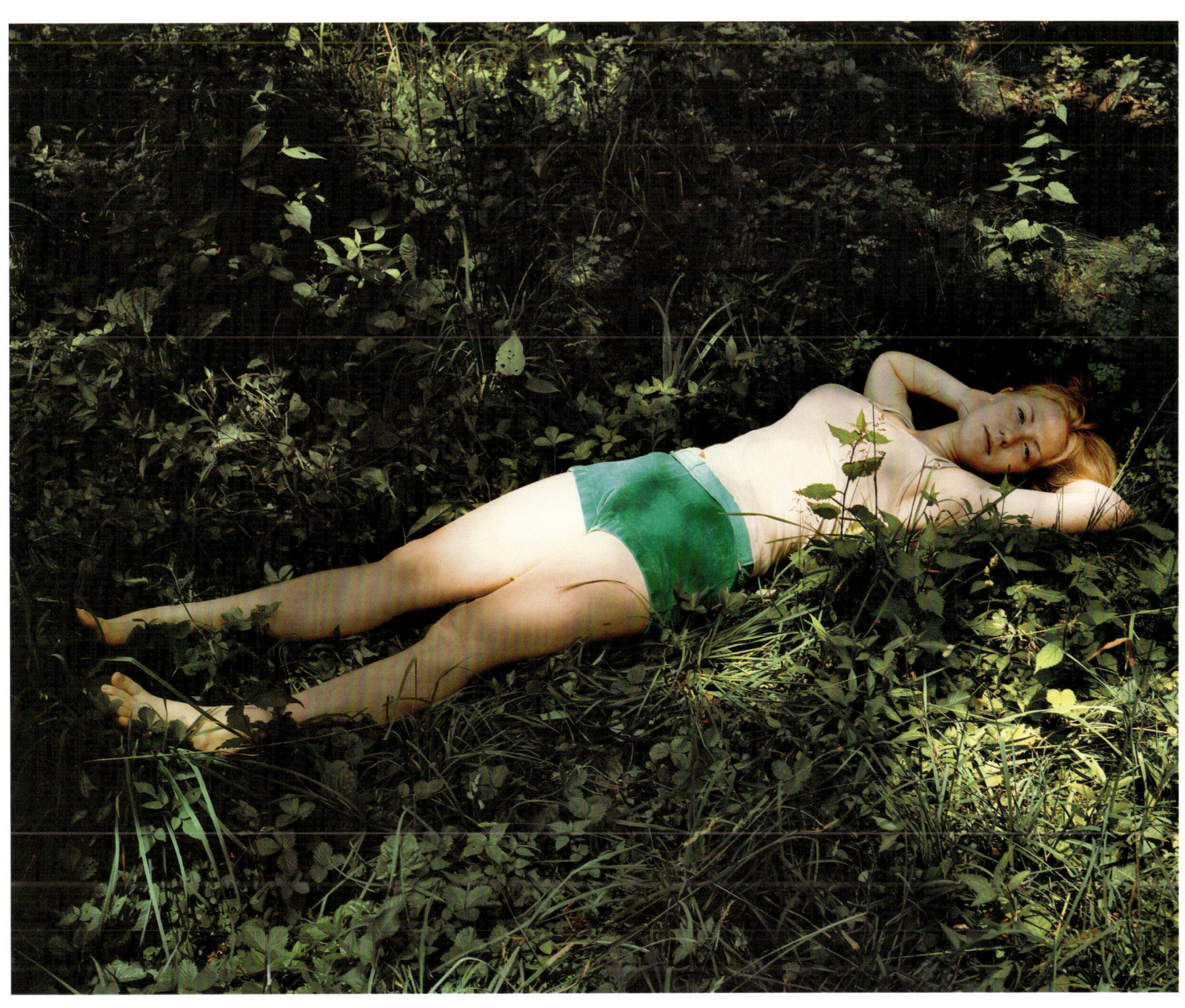

Sarah, b. 1984

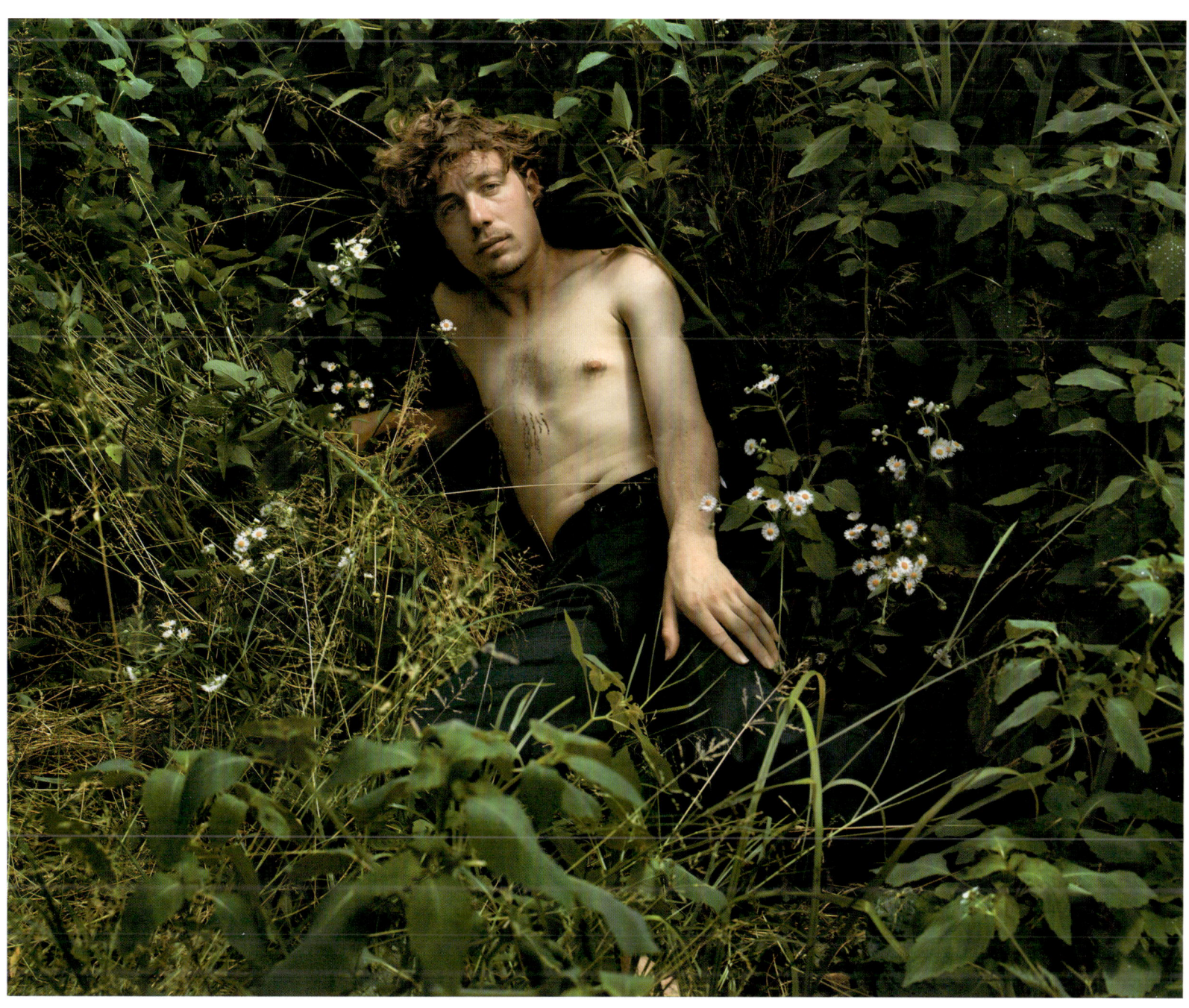

Brian, b. 1976

As a kid, I liked to sneak downstairs when we visited my great-grandmother's house. There was usually a body in the parlor. I'd stand nearby, enjoying the smell of fresh flowers and wondering about this stranger's life and what kind of person he or she was. It's hard to describe, but that feeling of inevitable loss is something that never goes away. I am still intrigued by strangers—the kind of people I see at the grocery store or sit next to on the train. I guess portraits are a way of honoring people that I hardly know but already miss. **KATY GRANNAN**, 2005

SOME OTHER PLACE THAN HERE
JAN AVGIKOS

Our times will be remembered as a period of chronic cultural sea change. In the blink of an eye the world transforms itself—and that on a regular basis. Today is not like yesterday; tomorrow will be even more radically different than today. Soon after that, life as we know it might well disappear. Together, we've survived the Y2K millennial shift, the disasters of 9-11, and a dizzying multitude of changes to daily life—all in the first half of the first decade of the twenty-first century. So much is compacted into so little time. We speed into uncertain futures, and we're breathless from the pace.

Do we not see ourselves in each other's eyes? No; the collective sense is that our differences are more pronounced than ever—on a par with the tumultuous sixties. What's more, our fractious, frayed state absolutely fascinates us and feeds our increasingly rapacious appetite for spectacles drawn from everyday life. Cultural difference as vicarious thrill is the engine that drives burgeoning forms of self-absorption and voyeurism at play in the American media, entertainment industries, cyberspace, and art alike. Straddling the yawning gap of the ever-widening social divide, up-close-and-personal formats are mirrored in the plethora of new reality TV shows; in one-on-one interviews that dominate the news and put a palpably human face on the hard cold facts of current events; in the booming business of celebrity culture (shop like a star, dress like a star, live like a star); and in mushrooming venues for pornography—all offering some fast and fleeting form of intimacy with strangers. Fueling the frenzy, the Internet teems with innumerable opportunities for social interactivity that efface distinctions between who we are and who we might envision ourselves to be. Playing host to virtual personas, who blossom online, are the myriad spaces of instant messaging, chat rooms, blogs, twenty-four-hour web-cams, gaming clans, and "shared-world" communities.

Rounding out the chorus that reflects and instrumentalizes our need to personify our relation to mass culture are the legions of real-life and fictional characters, with a full complement of quasi-autobiographical conceits and first-person narratives, who have been a mainstay in contemporary art for more than a quarter century. Nowhere are these tendencies more pronounced than in the photographic arts, as evidenced by Cindy Sherman, Jeff Wall, Nan Goldin, Larry Clark, Philip-Lorca diCorcia, and scores of other artists who began practice between the late seventies and the mid-eighties, mimicking and miming identity stereotypes as aggressively as they blur boundaries between reality and fiction.

Katy Grannan mines the fertile divide—social, economic, aesthetic—between us and them. Her portraits probe deeply into the underbelly of cultural difference, with an emphasis on personal values and contrasts between big-city life and the small towns and rural areas that exist far beyond the periphery of the center. The people she photographs are strangers to her, but the routes she travels—primarily from New York City to points in the Northeast/New England corridor—correspond curiously to her own personal road map. Born and raised in suburban Massachusetts and schooled in Pennsylvania and Connecticut, she lived and worked, until a recent move to San Francisco, in the heart of New York City. Her own experiences and identification with life in locales that stretch from the Hudson River Valley to Mystic Lake in Massachusetts, near her hometown, serve as a springboard to orchestrate encounters that supersede the so-called documentary impulse in photography.

There is no guise of objectivity in Grannan's art. Rather, her portraits are freighted with personal issues—hers, theirs, and ours—that emerge through the quasi-collaborative terms of engagement that she stipulates and that shape her interactions with her models. For a brief time, she and they become intimate strangers, mirroring each other's motivations and creating a drama that draws us in as the viewer and gives us a prominent role to play.

Anonymity is a pervasive, if not permanent, state in the sociology of Grannan's art. Typically, she puts brief ads in small-town newspapers, giving little information other than that she's a female photographer, who would like to photograph you in your home or surroundings, and her telephone number. The respondent must be not only willing to be photographed—in a private manner by someone who may or may not be who she says she is (a professional artist)—but also motivated enough to contact her and follow through with arrangements made over the phone. By identifying herself as female, Grannan enables her potential subject to make a series of assumptions: a female photographer might be more sympathetic than a male; inviting a female, rather than a male, stranger into your home might involve less risk of harm. Grannan is one of a number of young female photographers who began working in the mid-nineties and who use gender to inaugurate new genres and thematic directions in contemporary photography that would in all likelihood be off-limits to their male counterparts. The result is a cache of images of children, adolescents, teens, young adults, and trusting strangers—as in Grannan's work—who perform for the camera in ways that are at once scripted and quite candid.

These images require that we interrogate the subjective relations that sponsor "the shoot" and that might be said to prevail beyond the frame of the photograph. Such inquiries serve to arrest the mercurial boundaries between appearances and reality—no small matter when it comes to reading content. Just as we are compelled to question the social circumstances that couch Grannan's portraits, so, too, must we take into account the context in which we encounter her art. From the perspective of the rarified spaces dedicated to contemporary art that exist mostly in urban centers, the people and locales

she photographs stand out as ciphers of social difference and marginalization. At first glance, that might be all we can see. Yet, ultimately, whom we judge her subjects to be has everything to do with how much we're willing to acknowledge the ordinariness of our own lives and how much we're prepared to identify with people who decide, for one reason or another, to take Grannan into their confidence and to reveal themselves to a perfect stranger. Lest we forget—everyone has something to hide.

The idea of home is key in Grannan's work. In three series of photographs included in this monograph—"Poughkeepsie Journal," 1998, "Dream America," 1999–2000, and "Morning Call," 2001–2004—we encounter subjects in their own homes and, thus, gain access to certain aspects of their private lives.

It's notable that the one series for which Grannan chose to use black-and-white film—"Morning Call" (the series is named after the local paper in which Grannan's ads for models were placed)—began and was inspired by domestic spaces found in Allentown, Pennsylvania, the same town that Walker Evans photographed during the Depression. Given the shared circumstance of Allentown as the backdrop for both Evans's and Grannan's social investigations, and a straightforward style of portraiture that focuses unceremoniously on everyday people and the plain places in which they live, we're prompted to make transhistorical connections between then and now. Through Evans's and Grannan's images, we are given access to subjects who present themselves as individuals, and we're also afforded a glimpse of their world view. Pieced together from the evidence of their surroundings, the idiosyncratic constructions of personal space, and the vagaries of at-home demeanor, we are led to read into the portraits far more than we can actually see. We imagine the experiences of these subjects beyond the camera's range, beyond the close quarters of "home," and, in so doing, seek to discover the gestalt of the times, measuring cultural change incrementally, one person at a time.

Two subsequent series of photographs—"Sugar Camp Road," 2002–2003, and "Mystic Lake," 2004—shift outdoors, yet are within a close radius of home, in locations chosen by her subjects and embedded with personal meaning for them. Grannan works with her models collaboratively to decide how they want to be photographed. They make many of the decisions together: What will they wear? Will they be clothed or nude? What sort of poses will they strike? What do they want to reveal about themselves? Who do they want to be? "How comfortable are your subjects with the actual process of being photographed by you?" I asked Grannan in a recent conversation. We had been talking about what actually happens when she meets people for (what amounts to) the first and last time, excluding one or two phone conversations. I wanted to know what sort of apparatus they confront. She explained that she shows up without a crew, or even an assistant. She's as low-key as she can be, except for the fact that her setup demands a certain amount of support gear—primarily a tripod and lights. In addition she might use a fan, a stepladder, or other low-tech means to achieve the desired result. She also mentioned that she has an impression of herself in the process of setting up the photograph as physically a bit awkward, which she speculates might suggest to her subject that they share some sort of parity—an idea that's never far from my mind as we gaze upon her finished portraits.

In part, Grannan's methodology is old-fashioned. Using her 4-by-5-inch camera, with its specially ground lens and its upside-down image, the act of making the photograph is much more formal and traditional than hand-held, point-and-shoot photography. After she sets up the photograph, analyzing it from the camera's point of view, comes one of the most important parts of her process, when she steps away from the apparatus. No longer hidden behind the "box," as she puts it, she and her subject see literally eye-to-eye, a direct form of engagement that Grannan highly values and that serves as a matrix for the viewer's encounter with the portrait image.

We see plenty of awkwardness in the frozen poses her subjects manufacture for their official portraits by a genuine artist. Their discomfort is laced with a sense of familiarity, for we've all stood up to the camera and lost ourselves in the process. We recognize something of the exhibitionist in her subjects, and something of the voyeur in the artist and ourselves as well, each enabling the other. We understand at once that we are all roundly complicit in these matched sets of communicative acts. Her subjects perform not simply for the artist and the camera—they play equally to a much larger cultural arena as they strive to fulfill stereotypical expectations about beauty, virility, desirability, and success. Do we unwittingly reveal as much about ourselves as Grannan's subjects do about themselves? That question rims our reception as we examine the evidence of one person's life after another, as recorded in one fell shot through Grannan's lens.

Her images present us with many realities, not the least of which are the irrevocable consequences of living in mass America. We are far more influenced by the invasiveness of commercial visual culture and the pressure to conform than we want to admit. We compose ourselves according to ideas about what we should consume and how we should look and behave, in order to facilitate some image of whom we think we should be. We struggle to locate and maintain some sense of our own individuality, which many theorize is an outright impossibility given the grip of consumer culture on our psyches. Realism is written all over Grannan's photographs. Her knack

is that she manages to catch everybody (them and us) in the act of gearing up to be themselves.

In the series of photographs taken inside people's homes—"Poughkeepsie Journal," "Dream America," and "Morning Call"—Grannan uses domestic interiors to clue us in to the inner lives of her subjects. Cheap, dark-brown wood paneling is pervasive, as are drop ceilings, wall-to-wall carpet, miniblinds, and other features that scream "box store" décor. From one house to another, and from town to town, a picture emerges of the cloying dimensions and outright ugliness of generic America. Once inside her subjects' homes, Grannan reserves the right to intervene as stylist—to move things around, to rearrange the furniture, and to remove personal effects—with the result that the idea of home becomes far less cozy and inviting and far more institutional and sterile. This staging process might take up to half an hour, during which time her subjects prepare themselves for their big close-ups. By and large, Grannan says, people have given thought to how they want to be photographed and why, but over the course of the shoot costumes, poses, and props might change.

Her need literally to "get out of the house" precipitated her move from home environments to landscape settings in 2001. In "Sugar Camp Road" and "Mystic Lake," her subjects continue to exercise choice—she follows their leads, within general parameters that she establishes, as they select places that resonate with personal meaning; however, the stakes are radically altered with the move from private to public space. What people do behind closed doors and what people do out-of-doors are regulated by different sets of constraints, mores, and laws. It's okay, for example, to be naked in your own home, but it's a criminal offense in public. Many of Grannan's subjects opt to be photographed in the nude and to show themselves in a sexualized manner. Many of the pictures in "Sugar Camp Road" and "Mystic Lake" are edgy enough to suggest that if a state trooper had happened upon one of Grannan's photo shoots, it could have spelled trouble for her and her subject alike. We can imagine the list of possible charges—vagrancy, lewd and indecent behavior, perhaps even "solicitation." Working out-of-doors in the risky manner she prescribes calls for not only furtiveness but also a well-developed sense of defiance. She and her subjects might be strangers, but in the space of a single morning or afternoon, they're also coconspirators and partners in crime.

As developments in her art over a period of five or six years reveal, Grannan has become increasingly bold in orchestrating the social encounters that are the mainstay of her art. Earlier portfolios are composed primarily of images of young women much like herself. In "Poughkeepsie Journal" and "Dream America," more often than not, males are peripherally present as the children, siblings, friends, or lovers of the central female protagonists in her photographs. In her more recent series, "Sugar Camp Road" and "Mystic Lake," Grannan expands her repertoire to feature men—men who are middle-aged, who have big guts, who sport erections, who look as if they've seen better days. They aren't necessarily a pretty lot, yet all are willing to perform for the camera as well as the young female photographer who has invited them to express themselves to her in a private manner. This dimension of Grannan's practice is shocking! Think about it. No background checks. No safety of the studio. No guarantee that the bond of trust will be upheld. The situation is analogous to a woman hitchhiking by herself—she meets a few incredible people and lots of weirdos, too.

The increased risk factor delivers another jolt of realism to her work and spikes the level of vicarious thrill. There is nothing virtual about Grannan's encounters or her proposition to strangers to engage in acts of instant intimacy. In this respect, Grannan's art finds resonance with a group of female photographers that includes Rineke Dijkstra, Collier Schorr, Gillian Wearing, and Justine Kurland, among many others—female artists who mine the public domain in search of anonymous coconspirators to assist in hijacking social conventions in service of a theater of personal longing.

Grannan's subjects gaze at us with looks that approximate intimacy. What more could they deliver? None are professional models, and hence, they aren't all that experienced when it comes to staring down a big camera and holding the reins of how they want their image to look, particularly when they only have access to it in their mind's eye. How many selves must crowd into play for the hapless subject? How much programming gets regurgitated at the moment the camera clicks into action?

We see vacant stares that remind us of Manet's paintings of disenfranchised women, caught in the riptide of modern life. We see the melancholia of Cézanne's *Bather* in bodies that are more naked than nude. We see incarnations of nineteenth-century picnickers who seem stranded in the natural environment. We see film noir motifs in predatory camera angles, suffocating bowers, and deserted country lanes. Symptoms of displacement abound. Such disturbances are acute in Grannan's most recent work out-of-doors, in which bodies lie unprotected on the ground, kneel in swampy pools, recline by muddy puddles, and unabashedly "let it all hang out" in broad daylight.

We are suitably aghast as the camera turns on the subject, exposing its vulnerability, devouring its flesh, and reducing it to the sum total of its flaws. The camera's predatory regard is underscored by the hard perspectives Grannan builds into her pictures. Particularly in "Mystic Lake," she photographs from above, bearing down and hovering over the subject's body. Note how physically close she must be. Imagine how all this must

look from a distance: the sight of her up on her ladder, towering above her supplicant-like subjects. They submit to something they couldn't possibly have bargained for and respond with a leap of faith. Equal parts affection and predation—that's how Grannan describes what she sees in Garry Winogrand's photographs of women he all but stalked in pursuit of the pictures he wanted to make. She identifies with what she calls the "truth of the process," which necessarily involves the imposition of her way of seeing upon the people she photographs.

The truths these photographs embody also have to do with the defiance of her subjects to contradict the status quo, to take up with a stranger, to live dangerously, and to offer themselves up to the camera (no matter how uncomfortable) as a means of self-discovery. No wonder so many of her subjects look as if this is the most serious undertaking of their lives. What hangs in the balance has as much to do with attempting to apprehend oneself as it does with forestalling the utter anonymity that is, ultimately, the fate of us all. Death blankets our need to arrest time, and to memorialize ourselves before the fact of our own demise, in photographic images that are intended to outlive us and offer proof of who we once were. The willfulness of Grannan's subjects—to recognize the importance of representation and to go along for the ride with the artist, even if it feels like something they shouldn't be doing—is at the heart of what we champion in art. Make a record, make a mark, as a way to retrieve the past and link to future space. We are drawn into the stripped-down eventfulness of this moment as it plays again and again in Grannan's deeply humanistic art, with the result that the ordinary becomes extraordinary and our embarrassment gives way to absolute empathy.

JAN AVGIKOS is a contributing editor at *Artforum*. Her essays and reviews appear regularly in *Parkett* and *Flash Art*, among other international publications.

KATY GRANNAN b.1969
BIOGRAPHY

Born in Arlington, MA; lives in Brooklyn, NY and San Francisco, CA

EDUCATION
1999   Yale University, New Haven, CT, M.F.A.
1991   University of Pennsylvania, Philadelphia, PA, B.A.

SOLO EXHIBITIONS
2005   51 Fine Art, Antwerp, Belgium
        Fraenkel Gallery, San Francisco, CA
        Greenberg Van Doren Gallery, New York, NY
        Sugar Camp Road / Morning Call, Jackson Fine Art,
            Atlanta, GA
2004   Arles Photography Festival, Arles, France
        Sugar Camp Road / Morning Call, Michael Kohn Gallery,
            Los Angeles, CA
2003   *Morning Call*, Salon 94, New York, NY
        Sugar Camp Road / Morning Call, 51 Fine Art, Antwerp,
            Belgium
        Sugar Camp Road, Artemis Greenberg Van Doren
            Gallery, New York, NY
2001   *Dream America*, 51 Fine Art, Antwerp, Belgium
2000   *Dream America*, Kohn Turner Gallery, Los Angeles, CA
        Dream America, Lawrence Rubin Greenberg Van Doren,
            New York, NY

GROUP EXHIBITIONS
2005   *Some Body – Not Mine. The Beauty and Pain of Puberty*,
            Rudolfinum, Centre of Contemporary Art, Prague
2004   *Black & White*, Greenberg Van Doren Gallery, New York, NY
        Bucksbaum Award, Berkeley, CA
        Fifty One Celebrates Four Years, 51 Fine Art, Antwerp,
            Belgium
        From New York with Love, Covivant Gallery, Tampa, FL
        Land of the Free, Jack Hanley Gallery, San Francisco, CA
        Open House: Working in Brooklyn, Brooklyn Museum
            of Art, NY
        Whitney Biennial, Whitney Museum of American Art,
            New York, NY
2003   *Frankenstein*, Tanya Bonakdar Gallery, New York, NY
        Girls Night Out, The Orange County Museum of Art,
            Los Angeles, CA; Contemporary Art Museum, St. Louis,
            MO; Blaffer Gallery, the Art Museum of the University
            of Houston, TX
        Guided by Heroes, Z33, Hasselt, Belgium, curated by
            Raf Simons

*Imperfect Innocence: The Debra & Dennis Scholl
    Collection*, Contemporary Museum, Baltimore, MD;
    Palm Beach Institute of Contemporary Art, FL
Moving Pictures, Guggenheim Museum Bilbao, Spain
2002   *Boomerang: Collector's Choice II*, Exit Art, New York, FL,
            curated by Meredith Verona
        Casino 2001, Stedelijk Museum Voor Actuel Kunst Gent,
            Belgium
        *Dreaming in Print: Visionaire 10-Year Anniversary
            Exhibition*, Fashion Institute of Technology, New York, NY
        Installed Collections / Collections Installed, Mason
            Gross School of the Arts, Rutgers University, New
            Brunswick, NJ
        Legitimate Theater, Los Angeles County Museum of Art,
            CA, curated by Howard Fox
        The Norman Dubrow Biennial, Kagan Martos Gallery,
            New York, NY
        Smile, Here, New York, NY
        Tell It Like It Is, Diehl Vorderwuelbecke, Berlin, Germany
        True Blue, Jackson Fine Art, Atlanta, GA
2001   *Women by Women*, Cook Fine Art, New York, NY
2000   *Bluer*, Carrie Secrist Gallery, Chicago, IL
        Kohn Turner Gallery, Los Angeles, CA
        Reflections Through A Glass Eye, International Center
            for Photography, New York, NY
1999   *Another Girl, Another Planet*, Lawrence Rubin Greenberg
            Van Doren Fine Art, New York, NY
        Female, Wessel + O'Connor Gallery, New York, NY,
            curated by Vince Aletti
        P.S.1 Contemporary Art Center, Long Island City, NY
1998   A&A Gallery, New Haven, CT
        ArtSpace, New Haven, CT
        DFN Gallery, New York, NY

PUBLIC COLLECTIONS
Bard College, Annandale on Hudson, New York
International Center of Photography, New York
The Metropolitan Museum of Art, New York
The National Museum of Women in the Arts, Washington DC
The Orange County Museum of Art, California
The Solomon R. Guggenheim Museum, New York
The Whitney Museum of American Art, New York

FELLOWSHIPS AND GRANTS
2004   Baum Award for Emerging American Photographers
1999   Rema Hort Mann Foundation Grant

This book received generous support from:
Greenberg Van Doren Gallery, New York; Fraenkel Gallery, San Francisco; and Salon 94, New York.

The book is also supported by the Jerome Foundation in celebration of the
Jerome Hill Centennial and in recognition of the valuable cultural contributions of artists to society.

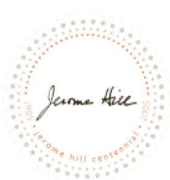

Acknowledgments

I am indebted to everyone who appears on these pages. Thank you for your trust, your generosity, and most of all for your fearlessness. These photographs were also made with the help and support of so many people. I am grateful to you all.

John McNeil, Ella Rose and Wyatt Lynch McNeil, William and Kathleen Grannan, Mary Ellen Grannan, Will and Beth Grannan, Connie McNeil, Jeanne Greenberg Rohatyn, Nick Rohatyn, Kim Le Liboux, Lesley Martin, Andrew Hiller, Jan Avgikos, Jeffrey Kane, Laurent Gerard, Gabe Greenberg, Olivia Marbert, Ronald Greenberg, John Van Doren, Dorsey Waxter, Sima Familant, Augusto Arbizo, Georgia Franklin, Amber Story, Paul Brainard, Carmen Hammons, Richard Ziello, Roger Szmulewicz, Tod Papageorge, Gregory Crewdson, Lois Conner, Richard Misrach, Jeffrey Fraenkel, Jerry Saltz, Deb Singer, Kathy Ryan, Jody Quon, Kira Pollack, Patricia Maloney, The Rema Hort Mann Foundation, Glen and April Bucksbaum, Kara Hamilton, Robert Lewis, Michael Kohn, Anna Walker, Malerie Marder, Katie Murray, Vicky Sambunaris, Michele Abeles, Honey Wade, Pinky, Betty, and J. M. (ad infinitum)

Special thanks to: Color Edge and Lexington Black and White NYC for printing, scanning, and pre-press work.

Front cover: Tim, b, 1981

Editor: Lesley A. Martin
Design: John McNeil and Kim Le Liboux
Production: Lisa A. Farmer

The staff for this book at Aperture Foundation includes:
Ellen S. Harris, *Executive Director*; Michael Culoso, *Director of Finance and Administration*; Nancy Grubb, *Executive Managing Editor, Books*; Andrea Smith, *Director of Communications*; Kristian Orozco, *Director of Sales and Foreign Rights*; Diana Edkins, *Director of Exhibitions and Limited-Edition Photographs*; Blair Knobel, *Work Scholar*

First edition
Printed and bound in Italy
10 9 8 7 6 5 4 3 2

Library of Congress Control Number: 2005923964
ISBN-13: 978-1-931788-81-6
ISBN-10: 1-931788-81-2

Aperture Foundation books are available in
North America through:
D.A.P./Distributed Art Publishers
155 Sixth Avenue, 2nd Floor
New York, NY 10013
Phone: (212) 627-1999
Fax: (212) 627-9484

Aperture Foundation books are distributed outside
North America by:
Thames & Hudson
181A High Holborn
London WC1V 7QX
United Kingdom
Phone: + 44 20 7845 5000
Fax: + 44 20 7845 5055
Email: sales@thameshudson.co.uk

aperturefoundation
547 West 27th Street
New York, NY 10001
www.aperture.org

The purpose of Aperture Foundation, a non-profit organization, is to advance photography in all its forms and to foster the exchange of ideas among audiences worldwide.